INTERIORS 3rd BOOK OF OFFICES

INTERIORS 3rd BOOK OF OFFICES

BY JOHN PILE

WHITNEY LIBRARY OF DESIGN
an imprint of
Watson-Guptill Publications, New York

The author wishes to express appreciation to the many designers, architects, planners, and firms who have provided the data and illustrations that have made this book possible. Every effort has been made to credit sources and photographers. In a few cases where illustrations have come from the author's own clipping file, credit information has not been available. A general apology is offered for any errors or omissions that may have occurred for this or any other reasons.

Copyright © 1976 by Whitney Library of Design
First published 1976 in New York by Whitney Library of Design,
an imprint of Watson-Guptill Publications,
a division of Billboard Publications, Inc.,
1515 Broadway, New York, N.Y. 10036

Manufactured in U.S.A.

Library of Congress Cataloging in Publication Data
Pile, John F
  Interiors 3rd book of offices.
  Includes index.
  1. Office layout. I. Title.
HF5547.P52   747'.8'523   76–20812
ISBN 0-8230-7305-X

First Printing, 1976

CONTENTS

PREFACE

The appearance of *Interiors 3rd Book of Offices* invites us to make some comparisons with the two earlier volumes in an effort to assess the progress of office design in recent times. In retrospect, *Interiors Book of Offices* by Lois Wagner Green, published in 1959, seems to sum up the arrival of the American post-World War II office. The era before the war now seems like a "dark ages" of the office. Of course, there were exceptions; Frank Lloyd Wright's famous Larkin Building and S. C. Johnson's office building are not only extraordinary buildings, but also conceptions of office work space that still seem viable today. (The Larkin Building, in spite of its modernity of concept, has, ironically, been demolished.) Lescaze designed offices for CBS, in connection with radio studio projects, that stand up well in relation to modern standards. In the main, however, the offices of the 1920s, 1930s, and 1940s were dismal and noisy warrens of black typewriters on olive-drab desks. These offices were divided into a maze of chambers by fencelike partitions and were clogged with overwhelming clutter.

Wartime industrial and corporate expansion, combined with stagnation in construction and renovation, led to a boom in postwar office design. The preexisting ideas of industrial designers, planners, and architects, which we usually call "modern," were ready for application in the kind of office that is organized for work efficiency—a setting to maintain or improve employee morale and express corporate (or other organizational) ambitions and ideals, all in one. The new profession of "office planner" or "space planner" emerged. One organization after another moved to "make a statement" through their headquarters and other offices that would catch up with postwar needs as well as symbolize modern ideals. This is the material of the "first book." Among the clients whose offices are described in this volume are Time-Life, Connecticut General, and Inland Steel; the designers are Gerald Luss at Designs for Business, Florence Knoll and the Knoll Planning Unit, and Skidmore, Owings, & Merrill. These were projects that broke new ground and established standards that are still with us.

The *Interiors Second Book of Offices*, edited and written by me, came 10 years later. During the decade that separates the two volumes what had been pioneering became routine. The "second book" bulges with photographs of innumerable projects, often seeming painfully similar and illustrating how the new norm spread throughout the business world. Dozens of manufacturers now offer office furniture to meet the modern planners' needs. Dozens of design firms are represented with work that would have been innovative just a few years before but which have now become commonplace. The outstanding projects, such as the Chase Manhattan tower or the CBS headquarters, represent both refinement of the art of office design and its maximization in terms of quality and massiveness.

Against this background of achievement, however, a few signs of forthcoming change are noted. Computers, hardly mentioned in the first book, had come on the scene with considerable importance by the time of the second book. Their new importance is reflected in the pictures of equipment, in the discussions of their major functions in large projects, and in the constant reference to them in the effort to assess what the future will bring. In looking through the pictures, one also feels that the abstractly "perfect" office interior has possibly reached its limit. There are references here and there to some new concerns about the seeming inhumanity of the vast projects, with their chilling emphasis on corporate supremacy. The individual office worker, always a small cog in a large machine, seems crushed within the gleaming elegance of the new corporate Versailles.

Along with the concern over the omnipresent slickness of the new office, a new departure appeared. It is discussed in a short chapter on a strange innovation known as "Office Landscape"—a European idea that was being described for the first time (which also appeared as an article in *Interiors*). More than anything else, it was the mention of this new and (to most of the established office design profession) alarming idea that marked the second book as a kind of watershed. Office planning as order, "cleanness," and elegance had reached its limits. A different approach was on the horizon.

The present volume is, in large part, a documentation of the impact of the "landscape" or "open plan" approach. No office planning is untouched by it; even absolute rejection of the concept now takes place only in full knowledge of what is being rejected and with careful consideration of the merits of one trend as compared with the other. The arrival and full acceptance of the computer as a key element of all office processes is not unrelated to this issue. Only the smallest of organizations, or those of a strictly professional character (such as law firms), are untouched by computers. The role of mass paperwork processing as the norm of office life has diminished to insignificance, while the office as a kind of forum for discussion and planning has grown.

Influences from the worlds of psychology, sociology, and what is usually called "human relations" combine with the growing role of unionism and assorted rebellions against established routine and authority (such as the women's movement) to conspire against the authoritarian-organizational office, with its emphasis on hierarchy, status, and the visible expression of these values. It is a curious paradox that the "landscape" idea originated in the service of essentially archaic, vast, paper-handling operations, but that its significance has increased precisely because of its usefulness in the *newer* kind of organization—one likely to be computer-dependent, more flexible, and more democratic than its predecessors.

Of course, it is dangerous to try to evaluate where we are now in relation to a more long-term process of change; it is often our very closeness to a process that makes it hard for us to analyze it. After allowing for that risk, however, it should be noted that this book deals with a period of change and reevaluation. The main emphasis of the postwar office as symbol, monument, and palace seems to have achieved its ultimate accomplishments and, in so doing, to have demonstrated its limits and its weaknesses. We are now in a more experimental period, one that is more dynamic and less certain of its goals. It is therefore probably more interesting in terms of process and development, but perhaps less rewarding in terms of clearly recognizable achievement. The new monuments that we can document, although even larger and more spectacular than those of a few years back, seem archaic — like fossilized survivors of the old period of unlimited optimism for the endlessly expanding gross national product.

Flexibility, informality, and the "ad hoc" approach are the current expressions of a failure of confidence in a clearly organized, tightly controlled, and endlessly profitable world. Search and experiment are in order again, and the office that best provides these conditions will have more relevance to current reality than the perfectly groomed and gleaming monument — however esthetically attractive that can sometimes be when executed by the most skilled design practitioner.

Modern technological civilization is, for better or for worse, shifting its emphasis away from the processes of production — factory and agricultural work — as these processes become more mechanized and more automatic. The role of human activity is changing from "labor" to control, from farm and factory work to office work. The office is changing from a specialized facility where a few "white collar" types exert control over all other human activity to a new situation where most work is "white collar." The office thus becomes the dominant place of work. It is only natural that this should mean offices become more varied, less stereotyped, and, it might be hoped, more appropriate settings for creative human activity than the power-centered office.

If the pattern of change in design is to continue, we must expect office design to become more diverse, more experimental, more contentious, and, in all probability, messier than the ideals of the 1960s called for. Only a few years ago, most designers thought of office design as "dull" because all the problems had been solved. Even if it is more problematic than in the recent past, office design has now exchanged dullness for the excitement of new explorations.

INTRODUCTION

It is almost always true that the most important and meaningful questions about any area of human activity are questions that are never asked, let alone answered. Everyone assumes that all those questions must have been satisfactorily answered long ago. We tend, then, to go on repeating familiar patterns of error on the basis of assumptions that we do not even know we have made. To look at the design of modern offices with any degree of sense, we first need to know what offices are for, what is done in them, why do they exist? The answers to such basic questions are amazingly difficult to find.

We all know that in any office, mail is opened and, we hope, read. Phone calls are received and made and a huge amount of typed or duplicated material is produced and sent out. To what end does all this take place and in what setting can it best be done? Any architect, planner, or designer who has been involved in the early phases of an office project has discovered how hard it is to find out what the realities of office operation are. Let us suppose that we will begin by interviewing each office worker, or at least the most important ones. They will surely tell us what they do and what their fellow workers do. We immediately find that the typical office worker believes that most of his fellow workers do nothing, or next to nothing. In fact he believes that many of them create problems and troubles that would not otherwise exist. When we try to discover what *he* does, this also turns out to be unclear. He is sure of its importance, but it is hard to pin down in words. If this is true of the modest clerical worker, it becomes increasingly true up the hierarchical scale through middle management to the top. The chief is least clear of all about what he does and is at a total loss about appropriate facilities. This is not to suggest that these people doubt their usefulness, nor should we necessarily doubt their usefulness. It is just that exactly *what* they do is not clear.

Every schoolteacher has heard conversations of the sort that run, "What does your father do?" "My father is a plumber. He fixes pipes." "My father is a carpenter, he builds houses." "Well, what does your father do?" "I don't know. He doesn't *do* anything. He works in his office." The last father may well concur in this judgment. What he does is so obscure, so abstract and formalized, and so built into a complex routine that it defies description in any reasonable, explicit terms.

C. Northcote Parkinson in "Parkinson's Law" takes on this situation through an elaborate spoof. Or is he perhaps serious, or at least quite factual, whether serious or not? "Work expands so as to fill the time available for its completion," he tells us. Office work seems to follow this rule with particular energy as we see in his statistics, which show us that while the number of capital ships in the British navy were declining by 67 percent, the number of clerks increased by 40 percent and the number of officials by 78 percent. Every office worker is aware that the paper he is producing is destined to be processed by other office workers. How much of his work is a net gain and how much is the processing of still other workers' work? No one seems to know the answers to these questions but we all know that the increase in an office staff of a given size does not produce an increase in any tangible output proportional to the size of the increase. An office staff of one is probably at the peak of its effectiveness. Two will not be twice as effective as one — with luck they may accomplish 50 percent more than the original one. Without luck the two may be less productive than one. No intelligent person would dream of claiming that 1,000 workers do 1,000 times the work of one. Half that would be a great achievement. The problem is, of course, that each office worker tends to spend time in dealing with his fellows. Part of this is inevitable (payrolls, organization charts, conferences, and meetings), and part of it is in the ills of office life (wasted time, power struggles, made work, and similar diseases).

However, in the end we must admit that offices have some use. It is attractive to propose a case for their total elimination, but we cannot really support the thesis that the world could work perfectly without any offices. Consider the situation of the firm (or the man) without an office. Work can be done, of course. Perhaps we are looking at a plumbing contractor. He works in the field installing bathrooms and furnaces. In his shop the necessary parts are stocked and prepared for installation. He must face several inevitable developments. He will receive messages. These may be notes, or phone calls, or even visits, but they will carry to him requests for his services, or instructions of a more specific nature about what is to be done. And then his crew of workers will need to be paid. The amount will depend on the terms of their employment (recorded where?) and the hours and circumstances of their work. The checks must be written (or the money counted into the pay envelopes) and then it will be time to get out the bills for the work done. These also require some information about the work done. How many hours of what worker's time and what materials were consumed? The bills must go out. Then it will become urgent to keep some check on who has paid up. The final question that will occur to him is, "Am I making money or losing it in this business?" He or someone else will have to do some figures to find an answer to this question. In fact, an office will begin to appear, located at first, possibly, in a coat pocket. Soon it will expand to occupy some little table or box, then to a desk. The desk will need to be enclosed and a file cabinet will join it. Soon, if the business grows, there will be more desks, more file

Schiller Building, 1891, Chicago. Adler & Sullivan, architects.

cabinets, typewriters, adding machines, a switch-board, more partitions, a waiting room, and even, if the firm really does well, a special building for it all. Another office project has developed.

The microcosm of office activity that we have described above is quite typical of all office work. There is really no useful work done in the sense of processing materials into products, transporting things or people, or otherwise satisfying the physicists' definition of "work." The functions of the office all have to do with two activities, which can be summarized as *communication* and *control*. Dr. Norbert Wiener in 1948 coined the word "cybernetics" for use as the title of a book he had written exploring, as his subtitle explains, "Control and Communications in the Animal and the Machine." He was primarily concerned, of course, with the rapidly developing uses of modern computers and their relation to human society. He needed one word to signify both communication and control, because these turn out to be the functions of the brain and the possible functions of the computer. It also turns out that they are (and always have been) the functions of the office.

As we think of communication and control, the word "control" quickly emerges as the dominating and powerful concept. Communication is only the servant of control, providing the data needed as a basis for action and carrying the controlling decisions outward to the functions that are being controlled. Control is the making of decisions in a form that will lead to their implementation. It cannot be effective unless communications supply the context in which decisions are to be made and the exact information about the specifics that are being controlled. Decisions turn out to be meaningless unless they can be conveyed into action effectively. The usefulness of a general in warfare depends on his communications. If they are cut off he ceases to exist for all practical purposes.

Until recently, decision making has been strictly a human function. In every situation there must be people who make the needed decisions as questions arise. Recently machines have appeared which offer to take over some decision making and we entrust many routine decisions to them already. More important and complex decisions remain a human province even though machines are offering more and more help in these areas. The most complex machines remain simple-minded when compared to the human brain and it seems probable that even as machines become more complex and subtle, some residue of key decisions will always remain purely human problems. Certainly policy making—the establishment of broad principles to guide everyday action and make more immediate decisions easier — hardly seems likely to become a computer function, however much the machine may help in this area. In any case, we

can say that as of now, control of any importance or complexity is exercised through people making decisions. A person can, of course, make decisions anywhere—he or she need not step into an office to do so. Where decisions are made by groups, the group can meet anywhere (on a golf course or in a restaurant, for example) and the decisions can be made then and there. Many office decisions are made, as we all know, outside the actual premises of the office. Why, then, do we connect decision making with the office at all? The answer must have to do with the other half of the definition of cybernetics: "communication."

A decision maker needs an address. We tend to assume that an address is necessary if a human being is to fully exist. Having no address makes a person suspect, or even illegal. He becomes a drifter and is in danger of being jailed (which at least gives him an address for the time being). A decision maker, or any person of any significance, must establish a location where he or she can be found. Even wandering prophets find it necessary to let it be known when and where they can be found, even if this only means a particular saloon or park bench. An effective decision maker in business, government, or any field of significant activity needs to have an established communication center where he can receive and send messages. When decision making becomes a group concern it is even more important that the members of the group have a way to locate one another and communicate as fully as may be necessary to the exercise of their control functions. We all understand that the address of a business is its main office (not its mine, factory, or showroom, unless the main office is combined with one of these) and all important communications must be directed to the main office. Both members of the organization and outsiders will also expect all important communication to come from that office. The factory manager waits for instructions from headquarters before he makes any important move. In many businesses we hear repeated phrases such as "we're waiting for word from upstairs" or "from New York" or "from 1450" (the last will turn out to be a street address where the decision makers are based) because the controlling main office has taken on the quality of a kind of oracle from which all significant decisions will flow.

Thus, an office is, primarily, a place for decision making. The decisions may be trivial and routine or basic and important, or both, but they require the support of communication both inflowing and outflowing. Inflowing communication will take the form of letters, reports, phone calls, punched cards, magnetic tapes, or other media; outflowing communication will use the same channels. But if we look more closely at these communications, we will find some more subtle distinctions. Both in and out communication will contain a large amount of data — simple information that is needed or might be needed in decision making at some time. But in addition, the arriving communication will include some proportion of queries and the outflowing communication will include some share of decisions (instructions or commands). Queries flow outward as well as inward, and so do instructions and commands, since there is no office entrusted with autonomous, total control of human activity.

Communication received cannot always be studied and acted on at the very moment of arrival, and decisions made cannot always be implemented at the moment of their making. Data is a kind of raw material that may be wanted at various times and must be kept available. One more function of the office thus appears which is only implied in the phrase "control and communication"; this is storage. Messages must be held and await their turn for action. Records or messages must be held for future reference, data must be at hand as needed for use in future decision making and action. The first and most basic data storage unit is the human memory, but we all know its limits and eccentricities only too well. As human activities become extensive and complex, no human memory or group of memories can serve the needs for information retention. Even a solitary individual finds that he must establish a file for his tax records, carbons of letters, lists of phone numbers, and similar simple data. A library is, in fact, a data storage device and so is a record collection or a roll of home movies. A business, government agency, or other sizable enterprise assembles data to be stored in staggering quantity, thus the problem of locating needed or useful data can also become overwhelming. Storage of data need not, of course, be physically located in the office. If communication with the data storage point is adequate, this function can be elsewhere. It is, perhaps, probable that our assumption that the office must house records will fade away as the development of more modern data storage and retrieval techniques lead to an office that can be *solely* a control and communication center uncluttered with archives.

If the discussion above seems vague and theoretical, it might help to look at a typical office in operation and try to tie its performance into the terms we have been using. Let us suppose that we look in on the main office of a small firm that manufactures hedge-clippers. We will surely find arrangements for incoming communication. These are the sense organs of the business. They will include the telephone switchboard, the letter slot (or its larger form, the mail room), and the reception room where callers present themselves. Arriving communications will either be stored (with some plan for retrieval at the appropriate time) or will be forwarded into a processing network. Data will be collated into forms for use either at once or

after a period of storage. Queries will move along a kind of assembly line where simple questions will receive routine answers (perhaps even automatically) and more complex questions will be referred upward to decision makers having larger fields of responsibility. The largest and most important queries such as "What is the future of this firm?" or "Whither are we headed?" may never be asked but will be implied in innumerable smaller inquiries.

Looking at specific examples of these various sorts of communication we might find:

Factory payroll records from last week arriving as printed sheets, punched cards, or magnetic tape. These are data to be stored for use in future reports.

Orders for hedge-clippers arriving from dealers or wholesalers. These are in fact queries (they begin, "Will you send me . . . ?") and they require only a routine decision to give a yes answer. The yes answer also requires that instructions move outward to the factory and that data about the order be stored.

A salesman arrives in the waiting room and asks to see a buyer of raw materials. His communication is also a query ("Will you buy . . . ?"). If he is fortunate his query will be stored in the form of notes, catalogs, quotations, etc., until a time of decision making comes along.

The factory manager telephones to report the breakdown of a piece of production machinery. His call is quickly handed upward to a decision maker who can propose solutions to the resulting problems of delay and can advise on repair or replacement of the equipment.

Meanwhile, decisions are being made and the resulting instructions and actions are flowing outward. The factory will receive word on the volume of production for the weeks ahead. Shipping labels will be produced for finished products. Paychecks will be written for the next payday and the annual report will be prepared for distribution to stockholders. All of this activity may be less tangible and less visible than the actual making of the hedge-clippers down at the plant, but it cannot really be said that nothing is being done.

We have used as an example here the office of a manufacturing firm because its activities are so closely related to visible production. Many other offices deal in matters far more abstract and removed from the easily comprehensible. Consider a stockbroker's office. It is certainly a busy place where fortunes can be made and lost, but it deals only in communications. The stocks and bonds are, themselves, merely printed messages and so are the checks or cash that pay for them. The whole operation is largely a message center where orders can be received and the necessary instructions collated and forwarded to the brokers on the exchange floor. Records must be kept so that the results of the transactions (which are also in the form of messages—statements or checks) can flow outward. The realities represented in this activity are remote and often hard to explain (as anyone who has tried to describe the securities business to a five-year-old will know), but they exist nevertheless.

In all office operations there is a certain observable hierarchy that moves from routine operations at bottom upward to unique and creative decision making at the top. At the low end of this scale we find the most basic, mechanical operations. A letter received is always opened; a ringing telephone is always answered; a letter dictated is always typed; a signed letter is always folded, stamped, and mailed. Many more important operations are almost as routine. An order is always filled, if possible; a worker is always paid at his standard rate for the hours he has worked. These are the tasks most easily mechanized and we find them becoming more the province of business machines and computers every day. Up the scale from such routines are more subtle decisions that must still be made every day. Should a job applicant be employed? The answer is, in a sense, routine since it is "If we need such a man and this applicant is qualified, yes," but the two "if" conditions are, as yet, beyond the ability of a machine to answer. Even now, however, a computer might process job applications in order to eliminate all but the few most promising who can then be referred to a human interviewer. Still more difficult decisions become the province of upper level executives or committees. These might range from daily complex questions such as "Where shall we open a new branch?" or "Shall we maintain, increase, or decrease the price of product X?," upward to vast and confusing problems such as "What plans shall we make to be ready for conditions next year, 10 years from now, or even 100 years from now?" Asking and attempting to answer such questions is, of course, "policy making," the highest level of executive activity. Successfully conducted, it establishes the guidelines that will make it easy to answer more immediate questions as they come along. To give top level attention to routine questions will waste the energy of an enterprise. Giving routine answers to (or omitting to ask) big questions will weaken its chances of survival. Organization in an enterprise is its method, its network of routing, to insure that every question is dealt with at the right level so that it will receive the best possible answer. Organization can only operate with the aid of its communication network and its data storage and retrieval system.

Organization is, of course, an abstract thing. It consists of titles, ranks, procedures, routines, routings, rules and regulations, and customs and habits. These things can all exist in people's minds alone, but a desire for stability, repeatability, and reliability makes it desirable to give these abstractions more tangible forms. Thus, an organization is usually an abstraction given concrete form in charts, diagrams, manuals, printed forms, memos, lists of rules, walls, doors, telephone wires, and other visible and workable organs. Many of these things could also work in an open field (as they must for an army in battle, for example), but it becomes convenient to shelter them from the weather, give them an address, and so on to create an office. The set-up of the office, it turns out, can be a highly important organ for organization, or, if it is badly conceived, for undermining organization.

A perfect office would be one designed to aid the most efficient flow of communication so that every decision would be made at exactly the right level, at exactly the right time, and with all the pertinent information brought to bear. Many circumstances in addition to the physical arrangements of the office are involved in bringing about such a state of organizational perfection. These include such diverse matters as the selection of personnel, the suitability of the abstract organization, and the quality of the equipment and systems for communication and storage of data. Together these things are, no doubt, more important than the office itself. Nevertheless, the office premises are a factor that can influence organizational performance to a larger degree than is often realized. Let us consider some examples.

One system of communication that remains in heavy use, in spite of all the attempts by technology to make it obsolete, is face-to-face conversation. Interestingly, it becomes more important as the level of matters communicated becomes higher. We are satisfied with a wire, a letter, or a phone call to convey a trivial message, but before we make a major decision we go to the significant people for a face-to-face interview if it is at all possible. Every office is the scene of endless conversations between members of the organization and between members and visitors. The physical set-up can make it easy to locate the people to be talked to or can make it difficult or troublesome. There can be the needed degrees of privacy or they can be missing. Proximity tends to lead to easy and full communication, while remoteness can reduce communication and introduce misunderstanding. Information can also flow on paper and is most often stored in this form (when stored in more modern forms, such as magnetic tape, it is usually still delivered on paper). The arrangements for paper handling in an office can make messages and data accessible when and where needed, or can lead to confusion, misdirection, and loss.

All of these practical considerations may be more or less obvious, although the design of most offices, including many that are the work of supposed experts, suggests that the obvious could use more attention. In addition, there are more subtle ways in which the office can influence the effectiveness of the enterprise it houses. For example, there are the considerations that are usually discussed under the designation of "human engineering." Until all office work is taken over by mechanisms, the people who carry on office functions will work best if conditions of work help rather than hinder them. This means that there must be enough light (not too little or too much), air at the right temperature and humidity, the right sound levels, work surfaces and equipment in the right places, proper seating, and the like. Innumerable experts are prepared to offer standards for each of these things, usually in connection with offering equipment for sale, but it turns out that the offered standards differ with one another and change from year to year. Even the application of all the most favored current standards does not guarantee that the individual office worker will find himself in a satisfactory working situation. In addition to being right, the working conditions must feel right to the person who uses them or must, at least, come as close as possible to this goal. This involves extraordinary subtleties. Seeing a window may be vital, even if it offers no light or view under certain conditions, while windowless space may be totally satisfactory in a different context. The typist who is deprived of a favorite picture or flower vase may become a liability to her firm instead of an asset. These personal and psychological considerations are probably far more important than is generally realized and are particularly hard to deal with because they are not as amenable to standardize as are matters of a physical nature, such as air temperature or light level.

There is a new recognition of some of these more intangible values, at least in some businesses, probably as a result of Madison Avenue's aggressive promotion of the concept of "image." Any public-relations-conscious business realizes that its offices, particularly those visible to the public, can be significant elements in building (or tearing down) the "image" that the firm wants to create. "Image" is not always to be equated with excellence, however. It is rumored that the General Services Administration of the U.S. government had a policy, for many years, of seeking out and creating offices of a particularly dreary, down-at-the-heel character that most of us would associate with the worst implications of the term "civil service." The idea is that the citizen stopping in to ask about a Social Security card or perhaps answering an invitation to talk over a tax audit would be outraged to find the government staff in comfortable, let alone attractive, quarters. The "image" sought in this situation was, it seems, exactly the dingy and depressing one usually achieved. Even government agencies are coming to realize that a more favorable physical setting may have favorable consequences through the reactions of visitors and it is certainly clear that no modern corporation with a forward-looking management is willing to neglect the cultivation of the favorable reactions that a well-planned and handsome office facility can bring about.

In theory, an office that will impress visitors favorably will also have a favorable influence on an organization's own staff. Most designers would admit, at least privately, that this is not always so. Many handsome and distinguished buildings, many office floors that have been widely publicized and honored for their decor, house workers and executives who have innumerable gripes and complaints. In fact, it sometimes seems that the complaints of the occupants rise in direct proportion to the excellence of the project from the designer's point of view. No one would claim that this is a healthy or natural situation and it surely indicates that the planners and designers of offices are overlooking some important concern.

If there is a general theme underlying the complaints that we hear about the supposedly well-designed office, it would seem to revolve around the feelings of its users that their rights to make their work situation suit themselves have been usurped. The designer emerges as a kind of czar or dictator who orders that things must be so. Only approved pictures may be hung; knick-knacks must be banished; beloved old furniture must be replaced with expensive and uncompromising new things. The designer is aiming at a unified and forceful visual statement and has the backing of authority. The staff (and executives too) often feel that they are being forced into a kind of uniform without their consent. The more successful the designers are in gaining their way through official edicts, the more likely they are to find themselves engaged in a silent war with the users of the project. The users, on the spot every day and with years ahead for their campaign, are usually the victors in such wars.

There are ways to make offices work well, to make them communicate a favorable visual impression and at the same time make them hospitable to the needs, real or fancied, of the individual to have things as he wants them. Establishment of rigid formulae is probably an easier route to a visual result that will photograph well and impress the casual visitor, but rigidity has a poor record of lasting power. Many of the sloppy, chaotic, and depressing offices that one visits today are the design formula achievements of a few years back.

History

Office design and planning is too new an activity to have any formal history. Office buildings show up in architectural histories only in the final chapters because no such buildings were built before the 1880s. Even after a history of office buildings has emerged, the offices within remain insignificant, so that we do not find many published references to them. Yet offices have certainly existed in some form for a long time. We are sometimes shown a space in an ancient castle or monastery and told that it must have been "the office." It is never more than a bare room. There are illustrations showing medieval monks at work on manuscripts sitting at rather carefully planned carrels that might now be called "secretarial work stations" or something of the sort. However, this is hardly office planning in the modern sense.

Some of the best descriptions of old office situations appear as incidental background in literary works. To speak of an office as "Dickensian" brings to mind a very definite picture based on highly realistic accounts of offices that Dickens saw. The notorious Mr. Scrooge of the *Christmas Carol*, for example, at the beginning of that famous story, sits in a "counting house" where it is already dark enough by three o'clock to require candlelight. His clerk sits in "a dismal little cell beyond, a sort of tank" where he copies letters. Scrooge and his clerk each have a coal fire but the clerk is allowed so little coal that his fire gives no heat—he uses his candle to help him keep warm. We feel sure that this office was simply a room in a small building that had originally been a house. Such offices are still common in London, although clerks probably can expect better treatment now, and candles are no longer the preferred lighting device.

In fact, the typical historic office was a room in a house. Before this developed, we can assume that the office in the coat pocket was the norm, but when a room became necessary it was most often a room in a house. Eventually it wasn't possible or sensible to live where the office was, and the office remained as a room in a house where no one lived. Such a house was soon filled with offices as the turn of events changed a formerly residential neighborhood into a business neighborhood. Actually, an old house serves fairly well as a small office building. It provides a number of small rooms and the necessary services in a way that gives a sense of comfort and informality. It is interesting to note that an old house is still often sought out for offices by many organizations that could afford more standard office space. Designers, architects, and office planners have a particular affinity for this kind of accommodation even now. It may be that the curious accidental possibilities of such a space have some particular appeal to creative people. In any case, many offices are still in converted dwellings and many ideas about offices must surely have their origins in this situation.

In *Life with Father*, Clarence Day describes an office of the 1890s that must have been established in a converted dwelling. His account is worth repeating:

"We came to a neat but narrow five-story building and walked up the front stoop. This was No. 38 Wall Street. Father's office occupied the ground floor, at the top of the stoop, and on the back part of the second floor he had a small storeroom.

"The office was busy in what seemed to me a mysterious way. The cashier, who never would let me go inside his cage, sat in there on a stool, with a cash drawer, a safe full of books, another safe for securities, and a tin box full of postage-stamps which he doled out as needed. One or two bookkeepers were making beautifully written entries in enormous leather-bound ledgers. They had taken the stiff white detachable cuffs off their shirt-sleeves and stacked them in a corner, and they had exchanged their regular jackets for black alpaca coats. Future bookkeepers or brokers who now were little office boys ran in and out. Western Union messengers rushed in with telegrams. In the front room there was a long table full of the printed reports issued by railroads about their earnings and traffic. . . . On or around the table were . . . a blackboard, a ticker, and four or five whiskery men.

"Father went into his private office where a little coal fire was burning, hung his hat on a rack, and unlocked and sat down at his desk. While he opened his mail, I proudly brought in two stone jugs of ink, one of greenish black made in England and one to use when he wrote letters of which he wished to keep copies, because with this ink impressions could be taken to put in his files. I cleaned and filled all Father's inkwells, and put fresh steel pins in his penholders. He had quill pens at home, but he used only steel pens at the office, and as he had no stenographer, he wrote a good share of the firm's letters in longhand himself.

"There were lots of things to do in the office besides filling inkwells. It was fun to scamper around the streets carrying all the messages (which are telephoned nowadays), or to roll coloured pencils down the clerks' slanting desks, or try to ring the bell on the typewriter. The latter was a new contraption which seldom was used except on important occasions, when the bookkeeper or one of the office boys had to stop work and pick at it."

The converted house that Mr. Day, Sr., occupied probably served him quite well. The pressure for something else did not arise out of the internal demand of the office—it came rather from the inability of the city to meet the demands for office space. Houses are usually no more than three or four, at most, five stories in height. As long as offices occupy converted dwellings, there is a clear limit to the density and concentration that is possible. The office tenant desires,

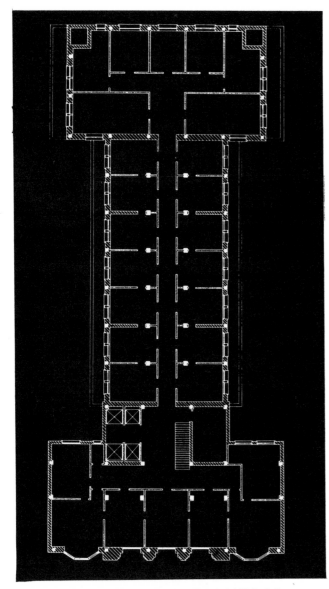

The hotel-like plan of an office building of 1891. Adler & Sullivan's Schiller Building in Chicago.

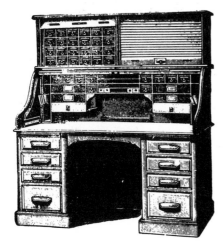

From the *Scientific American* of March 15, 1890.

in most cases, not only space for his firm's functioning, but also a location that is sufficiently close to some particular focus of activity.

It is true that the importance of face-to-face contact is constantly diminishing as the excellence of communication systems develops. There are, nonetheless, still foci of communication — some as clear as the stock exchanges, others more vague neighborhoods where certain specialties congregate — which tend to group offices in confined geographical areas. These are usually areas that had been residential in the past, and the buildings had to serve as offices when businesses moved into the district. However, office occupancy tends to make a stronger demand for concentration than does residential occupancy. In strategic neighborhoods, the available buildings fill up and it becomes clear to the landlord that he could rent more space than he has available in the preferred locations. Rents and building values rise under these circumstances, but it also becomes clear that office buildings could accommodate businesses better than converted dwellings ever could.

In Chicago it is easy to identify the early buildings constructed solely for office use. They are in the business district and are high enough to need elevators. The invention of the elevator occurred conveniently early, making this device available when the office buildings began to move into the old business districts where the existing low converted buildings could not keep pace with the demand for office occupancy. Offices appeared in other places as well, in factories and stores, wherever the size of a business grew to the point where vest-pocket offices or home offices ceased to be adequate. At first, the typical pattern was for the office to be makeshift—a small corner set aside and then later partitioned, but really still just a corner of the shop. Such offices are still common in small stores and industrial plants. The planned office building connected with a factory or warehouse appeared around 1900 to serve the giant company, which only became common as mass production and mass distribution systems developed. It was usually not in the heart of a city business district, and so was less likely to be a tall building.

The early office buildings of large cities such as Chicago and New York had much in common with buildings that are built now. In New York the external design was often quaintly nostalgic, but in Chicago it was often superior to the average buildings executed since. Internally, however, these older buildings provided office space almost exactly like that in the converted dwellings that were their predecessors. An office was a room and an office building was simply a vast honeycomb of rooms. It is fascinating to learn that when Adler and Sullivan were designing the famous Schiller Building in Chicago, the clients were uncertain whether the building should be an office building or a hotel and so instructed their architects to plan a building that could be used for either purpose. Adler and Sullivan apparently saw nothing odd about this—either use required nothing more than corridors lined with rooms plus stairs, elevators, and toilets. The building ended up being an office building, but a glance at the plan of a typical floor shows that a hotel would not have been very different. If an office tenant needed more than one room, he simply rented several side by side, as a large party will now rent a block of hotel rooms. The public corridor served as circulation for public and workers alike.

The room, the private office itself, as the basic element of office occupancy, reflects the origins of the office as a study or library in a home or as a work cubicle partitioned off from a shop. A man went into his office for privacy and to have the records at hand that he needed. His *work* was likely to be done outside, however, in the exchange, in court, or in the shop. The office was merely an address, a place to write letters and keep books. Even today this might be typical of a real estate broker in a rural community or of an insurance agent working in a small town. We must also remember that the early office was untroubled by the telephone and that with no typewriter, letters were written by the sender (or possibly copied by a clerk). The typical desk of 1850 or 1860 reflects this orientation toward solitude and privacy as the office climate. A man faced into his desk and confronted pigeonholes and drawers. Callers were few and he turned to speak with them. There was no secretary to take dictation since women did not appear in the office until the typewriter and its adjunct, shorthand writing, introduced this possibility.

The early business office probably served a firm that was a "sole proprietorship," that is, had one owner or a partnership. The offices only needed to seat the owner, or partners, and the staff, which usually consisted of a few clerks and a boy. Accounts were kept in books and the files tended to be small, since the production of handwritten letters and copies was modest. It was the appearance of the modern corporation and its parallels in modern government that produced the modern concept of offices as a complex grouping reproducing the organizational hierarchy of the firm in its layout of spaces. The quantities involved in mass production and mass distribution create a matching volume of clerical operations and the typewriter and the adding machine are essential. The offices of such large businesses take on similarities to factories with rows of office workers mass producing the paper that relates to the organization's products or services. Small rooms are poorly suited to housing such operations and thus the "general office" or "pool" appears.

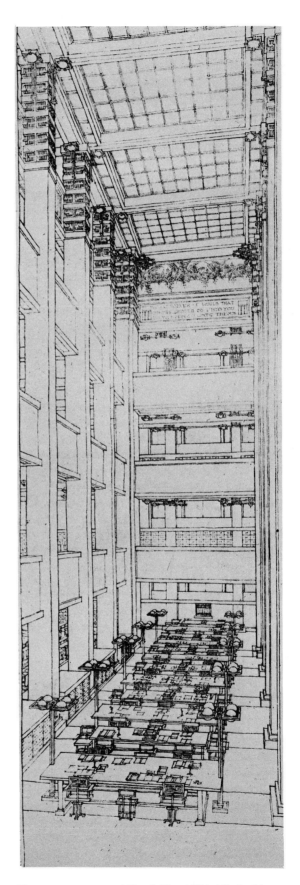

The central space of Frank Lloyd Wright's Larkin Building, 1904, in Chicago.

Mies van der Rohe's glass tower project of 1920–1921.

Walter Gropius and Adolph Meyer's competition drawing for the Chicago Tribune office building in 1922.

Although the earliest tall office buildings often seem quite modern in architectural concept, because they were in city "downtown" districts, they rarely made much provision for large office spaces. Their tenants were mostly to be brokers, agents, lawyers, and others who needed, or were content with, the old type of individual rooms. Indeed, even now the buildings in the heart of a city are often filled with such accommodations. The offices of large firms, corporations, insurance companies, mail-order houses, and government agencies are more likely to be away from the extremely high-rent districts, perhaps near the factory or in a smaller and less congested city. Such buildings, since they seldom need to be high, are less spectacular in modern architectural design. Wright's Larkin office building of 1905 is one fine example of the architectural possibilities of this kind of office group, but it is difficult to think of other examples to put beside it until we come into the 1930s and 1940s.

High buildings in America did not follow up the promise of the early Chicago skyscrapers, so that skyscraper history is largely a catalog of architectural absurdities. In Europe, Corbusier, Mies van der Rohe, and Gropius all produced designs of office buildings that would have been distinguished if built, but none of the projects materialized. These projects, nevertheless, had vast influence on architectural thinking and deserve to be studied as fully as any actual buildings. Mies designed several glass skyscrapers in 1919, 1920, 1921, and a large concrete office building (although not tall by modern standards) in 1922.

Any one of these projects would be a distinguished building if constructed now. Mies' own recent work with high buildings is perhaps the clearest realization of the promises of his early schemes. Gropius, with Adolph Meyer, entered the compeititon for a design for the Chicago Tribune Building in 1922 with a proposal that is also superior to 98 percent of what is built now. The fact that the winning design (which was built) was one of the most extreme absurdities of the pseudo-Gothic skyscraper mania served, with the passage of years, to draw more attention to the essential soundness of Gropius' design. It is possible to regard Corbusier's design for the Palace of the Soviets in Moscow as an office building, although it serves other functions. It was actually built in 1929, but constructed without proper architectural supervision and in a place where it was inaccessible to most Western travelers. The building itself had less influence than the architect's masterful and widely published drawings. The unbuilt design for an insurance office building in Zürich in 1933 is a clearer example of Corbusier's approach to the problem.

The first fully modern tower office building to be constructed anywhere was the Philadelphia Saving Fund Society Building (PSFS) put up in that usually conservative city in 1932 by William Lescaze and George Howe. Lescaze had brought the best of European thinking with him when he came from Switzerland in 1929 and managed to persuade the bank and his previously conservative partner Howe to embody these new ideas in a large building that still ranks as one of the best tall buildings. Certainly, it is the best building before the late 1940s in the U.S. Since this was also a building for mixed tenancy in a congested central city district, it was planned to accommodate the tenants' need for division of space into innumerable small rooms. This was done with movable partitions rather than with fixed walls so that flexible planning to suit the particular tenant was made possible. The partitions of the PSFS building were designed for that project, but the idea had been in use for some time. Such partitioning was probably first developed to make it easy to create makeshift office in a factory or store, but the developers soon realized that the flexibility of such partitioning could also have advantages for office building tenants and owners. Most early systems resulted in a distressingly grim appearance, but the system developed for the Philadelphia building made it clear that movable partitions could be trim and presentable.

Most of the large skyscraper projects of the 1930s and 1940s made some effort to offer building-standard systems that would permit some degree of flexibility, but it remained clear that owners and architects were still, in most cases, thinking of office buildings as warrens of many more or less identical individual-room offices. When large companies moved into such buildings they could arrange to have all partitioning left out where open, general office space was desired. Planning was a matter of open spaces plus cubicles. Perhaps there would be a waiting or reception area with more pretensions; and often upper ranking executive offices and board rooms would receive an interior decorator's attention in the form of pseudo-Georgian paneling and furniture.

Post-World War II developments brought together the ideas that were hinted at in the most advanced projects of the 1920s and 1930s. New buildings created a vast acreage of new office space, part of it built as real estate speculation (or "development," to use a kinder term), part of it built by businesses and government for their own use. Almost all this new building was modern in architectural concept (although often poorly designed) and the need to plan the facilities that were being built so rapidly created a new field of professional office design. The practitioners included architects, interior designers, industrial designers, and a variety of new types of specialists who called themselves office planners, space planners, or office planning consultants in an effort to identify the specialized nature of their work. Suppliers of furniture, partitions, floor coverings, and other components of the typical office were also tempted to enter this field in order to help their customers and help themselves capture orders for their products. Although the nature of such services makes them captive to a particular manufacturer or dealer, it is a surprising fact that, in at least a few cases, these services have done work of outstanding quality.

The 1950s seemed to have produced a well-established character for the modern office, but any sense of unchanging standard norms must now be put aside. Two powerful changes have had their separate and combined impacts on the modern office. The first of these has been the sweeping acceptance of the modern computer for a vast range of office tasks. After an initial period of experiment and uncertainty, electronic data processing has become the norm for any office task that involves repetition of operations in mass. The first reflection of the computer's arrival on the office scene was usually the reduction of clerical "pool" areas in which routine work had been done and the appearance of the "computer room"—a large and technically complex area in which the new machinery could be housed. The physical reality of the computer has become less intrusive in recent years with the arrival of remote terminals that make access to distant computers easy and with the appearance of more compact computer equipment. The reduction in clerical pools continues, but is balanced by the need for new kinds of office space for the programmers and other specialists who serve computerized operations. This is a new breed of office worker, neither clerical nor executive in the usual sense, requiring a special sort of work space still in the process of development.

A second development, partly coincidental and partly related to the "computer revolution," has been the invention of a new approach to office planning, sometimes called "office landscape" or "open planning." This approach sweeps away the conventional ideas about private executive offices and open pools and substitutes a more flexible use of space without dependence on fixed architectural elements. It is an approach that was at first highly controversial and is still open to continuing debate, but the impact of the idea has been so strong that almost every current office project is influenced by it in some way. Certainly the material in this book reflects an intense interest in this concept on the part of office planners during the last 10 years.

Office planning and design remains a somewhat confusing field. A typical project includes skills that were traditionally the province of the separate specialities of architecture and interior design, but it also can involve knowledge of office management and organization, office equipment (which becomes more

(Above) An office land-
scape: John Hancock,
Boston. Photograph by
Phokion Karas.

(Right) Office building for
John Deere & Co., Moline,
Illinois. Eero Saarinen &
Associates, architects.

complex every day), and industrial and advertising design vocabularies. The architect is theoretically the logical person to organize such projects, but most architects are so exclusively focused on the overall design of buildings that the many small and irritating problems of the offices within do not attract them. Traditional decorators and their newer cousins in interior design are inclined to concentrate on the superficial appearance aspects of the space they are concerned with. The ideal office planning organization is likely to include people trained in each of these specialties, but to have a focus on office work methods and flow, a special knowledge of office planning problems is necessary. Such expertise is essential to concentrate on these problems, however complex and troublesome they may be. This may be another case of modern over-specialization, but unless the generalists of design (architects and designers) can focus their time and attention on the office problem, the specialist will surely continue to be best able to secure office design commissions and carry them through to the satisfaction of the typical client.

Architecture

It might seem to be a basic reality that the architecture of office buildings would be a controlling factor in the nature of the offices inside. Actually, to a degree quite disturbing to architectural critics and theorists, offices are surprisingly independent of the buildings that house them. We find excellent offices inside bad buildings and poorly designed offices inside good buildings; we find old-fashioned offices in modern buildings and modern offices inside old buildings. This is a situation that speaks well for the flexibility of modern office installation materials, but raises some disturbing questions about office building architecture.

Every architect will agree that the inside of a building is fully as important, if not more important, than its external form. If architecture is an art of space, internal space is at the very heart of what architecture is about. Nevertheless, the fact of the matter is that the modern office building is rarely of much interest in spatial terms. We look at such exceptions to this rule as Wright's Johnson Wax Administration building as an illustration of what is possible. The big and famous skyscraper buildings of major cities are, almost without exception, exercises in the design of external mass. If they were solid masses, they would lose nothing in architectural character. The space within is simply a layer cake of uniform, characterless space. If led into an internal space blindfolded, even the most knowledgeable architectural scholar could hardly recognize more than two or three buildings by their internal design. Office buildings outside of cities (free of the pressures of high land values and restrictive laws)

The typical city office tower of the 1960s.

seldom do much better. We might guess that we were away from the city because of the slightly more generous use of space, but one building would be very hard to distinguish from another. There are exceptions, of course. Saarinen's IBM Research Center at Armonk or the American Republic Insurance Building by the Skidmore office come to mind, but it is not easy to expand this short list by more than a handful of other buildings.

This is not to say that one could not recognize certain office interior projects, the offices of certain companies, or the work of certain designers. The point is rather that the offices are, in most cases, little related to the building's basic design in any necessary and inevitable way.

This situation, however disturbing it may be to design critics, has its origins in valid realities and has some advantages to offset whatever we may think its disadvantages. The fundamental reality that has given character to office buildings is the nature of the real estate business. In our society, land is a commodity and its value fluctuates with supply and demand like any other commodity. Trading and speculation are possible and skillful dealing can produce huge profits (or, under certain circumstances, spectacular losses). Most office buildings are built when it becomes clear that the demand for office space in a given location is outrunning the supply. The land in any such location can generate rental income proportional to the size of the building that is on it. A large building will make more money than a small building. In such a situation, it is obvious that economic pressure will tend to urge the building of the maximum structure that the site can hold. The limit on size is, in reality, established by such practical considerations as the need for elevators, stairs, and structural support. These things increase as the height of a building increases and eventually will consume so much space on lower floors that the adding of upper floors becomes pointless. With modern structural techniques and elevator speeds, these limiting factors are often so insignificant that a building could be economically sound but also so huge as to create intolerable urban problems of street congestion, limitation of light and air, etc. In fact, these problems *are* created by the density of building in most center city areas. Legal restrictions through zoning laws appear only after such problems have become manifest and the laws, in order not to discriminate against the owners of property not yet developed, are usually excessively lenient. However, such laws are, in most city areas, the only effective limitation on building mass and density.

Buildings large enough to fully exploit the value of land up to the limits of the law and economic practicality are almost always far too large for any one occupant or owner to fill. They must be designed, therefore, as rental space suitable to any office tenant. Floor area becomes a commodity, just as land is a commodity, and the office tenant can lease space by the square foot just as one can buy sugar by the pound. Convenience in renting and in planning to accommodate the individual tenant depends on the floor space being uniform, and from the point of view of the agent, it is a convenience if space is uniform in all buildings. Any special characteristics or unique qualities in an office building become troublesome and, even if they may be advantageous, may be dimly regarded by real estate developers.

Certain concepts of modern architectural theory have worked into the real estate developers' concept of the perfect office building. The concept of "universal space" exemplified most clearly in the buildings of Mies van der Rohe, for example, places a high esthetic and intellectual value on space as a uniform, unbroken aspect of a building interior. Rooms, as such, become limiting and harmful to the modern architect's sense of his buildings; internal reality is seen as an open unit. Flexibility, a most modern virtue, is characteristic of "universal space" and is one of its chief rational justifications. The architect and the real estate developer thus find that they are in harmony in a desire to produce office buildings that are similar to factory and loft buildings in that they provide floor space, shelter, and necessary services, and nothing more. The architect would probably, in most cases, hope that the tenants of his building would want to preserve the open internal space with a minimum of obstruction, subdivision, and room building. However, the tenant is in fact free to use or misuse "universal space" as he may choose. If he wishes to have private offices and a board room that appear to have been transported from a Georgian mansion or a Louis XIV chateau, these can be created in "universal space" quite as easily as can the best of contemporary offices.

Some city buildings are built in part or whole for an owner tenant. In such cases the pressure of economics toward uniformity is often reduced (for example, at Lever House in New York), but the pressure still exists. The building must be financed, it must justify the taxes to be paid; a building that departs too far from the norm appears as a poor risk to lenders and can become a troublesome problem to its owners. Buildings built in suburban and rural areas escape from some of the inexorable pressures of the city real estate business, but here also certain cautions and habits work so that the departures from standard norms are usually limited and modest.

If we observe the pressures on the design of the typical urban office building, it is no surprise that such buildings tend to fall into a rather limited pattern. The project is, basically, a financial speculation with the aim of producing a maximum return on a minimum investment. The site is assembled by buying land that is vacant or occupied by buildings that earn less than the new building will earn for the same area. The site stops at streets that cannot be closed, at neighboring buildings that are too valuable to demolish, or at neighboring properties that cannot be bought by reason of their owners' stubbornness or excessive price demands. The zoning laws then establish for the site in question a set of limits on land coverage and height. These limitations can be complex, but the logical interpretation of the law will always generate an economic maximum of a specific mass. Everyone is familiar with the ziggurat-like setback pattern that resulted from the early zoning laws that required a building mass to stay within a sloping line plotted by rule. While such rules derived from a logical desire to limit size while maintaining maximum light and air for street areas, the rigidity with which they forced a building form that had no merits of its own, has led to their replacement by more flexible height zoning. The "area rule" method, for example, simply controls the floor area of the building as a multiplier of the land area. A building in a "4x zone" can have an area of no more than four times the area of the unbuilt land. Thus, it can cover the whole lot to a height of four stories, cover half the lot to a height of eight stories or take any other form that will keep within this restriction. Although this type of zoning gives more freedom to the architect in establishing the form of the building, the sensible possibilities will usually turn out to be quite limited.

A minimum number of stairways for safe exit are established by law. Minimum numbers of elevators and toilets to give an adequate standard of convenience are set by an interrelationship of legal requirements and economic pressures that rule that standards must match those of competing nearby buildings, while rents asked must also remain competitive. Construction cost is also influenced by architectural decisions about height and form and the resulting requirements for stairs, elevators, and structure. All of these factors taken together do not quite dictate building design, but they influence it with a hand so heavy that the architect's free decisions tend to be few and minor. If the resulting building creates an urban problem—visual, practical, or both—neither architect nor owner feels any particular responsibility. It is all too obvious that if they do not build the maximum building for the site, the project will die and a less scrupulous team will move in to take over. It is easy to be critical of the dullness and monotony of most modern office buildings, but it is not easy to propose a line of escape from the pressures that bring them into being. Creative city planning with strong legal and political backing has helped matters in some cities (Boston and

Philadelphia come to mind), but even in these situations the individual building is often unimaginative. At least a sound city plan, combined with progressive zoning, makes better office buildings possible when owner and architect have the imagination to take advantage of what is possible.

No matter how it has come about, whether it is a new building or an old one, the office planner confronts the building as a whole within which he must work. What are the considerations that limit what can be done? The list is surprisingly short and simple:

1. The basic shape and dimensions of the rented area.

2. The location of access (elevators and stairs) and services.

3. The size and spacing of columns (if any).

4. The location, spacing and shape of windows, and the nature of the light and view they provide.

5. The height of the ceiling.

Such other considerations as the nature of materials and finishes for floor, walls, and ceiling and the type of lighting are usually up to the tenant and planner, although a few buildings impose standards on items that might be visible from outside (window coverings or lighting near windows) or from public halls (walls and doors). The architecture of the building also influences the total sense of the tenant's occupancy through such things as the nature of the external appearance, the character of lobbies, elevators, and corridors, and, in some cases, the qualities of surrounding spaces to the extent that the architects have preserved parts of the site as open land. A few buildings offer more than the standard norm, but the vast majority adhere to a standard so consistent that the choice of space is more a matter of convenient address and availability of suitable area than anything else. Older buildings are, from the internal point of view, little different from newer ones. They suffer in competition only because they are frequently in less fashionable locations or have entrances and lobbies that seem dated.

Even if the list of basic architectural influences on office space is short, it is not negligible; every planner knows that different spaces under consideration for a certain tenant can vary greatly in suitability. Some of the variation follows a pattern and some is fortuitous and unpredictable. If we review our list in reverse order we will find:

The height of ceilings, if adequate—8 feet/2.45 meters or more—is of little importance.

More windows are always better than fewer, and large windows are usually better than small ones. This is

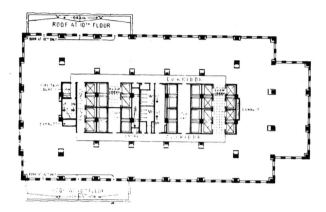

Plan, International Building in Rockefeller Center, New York. Reinhard & Hofmeister; Corbett, Harrison, & MacMurray; Hood & Fouilhoux, 1935.

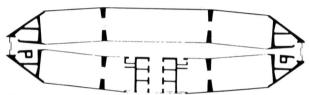

Plan, The Pirelli Building, Milan. Ponti & Nervi, 1956.

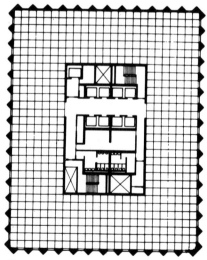

Plan, CBS Building, New York. Eero Saarinen, 1966.

because light and view continue to be highly valued, both for their real practical value and for psychological reasons that range from the symbolic to the absurd. In any case, it is easy to block off windows where they are not needed, but impossible to create them where they do not exist.

Fewer and smaller columns are better than many large columns. No columns is an ideal that many new projects approach. Actually, the presence of columns is usually quite easy to deal with successfully, but an absence of columns cannot present any problem at all.

Basic shape and location of access is somewhat unpredictable in its bearing on any given set of needs. In a general way, it can be said that simple block plan shapes are more flexible in office planning, but odd and tortured shapes can often be used well by a creative designer. The planner must usually make trial plans to test the suitability of a given space for a given use. However, there seems to be no virtue in the deliberate introduction of complexity of form in office building plans.

There have been a number of efforts to define more exact criteria for the intelligent, functional design of office buildings. These efforts seem to have two recurrent patterns. The first tries to establish a logical, ideal, basic floor plan in terms of building shape and core location. The second tries to work from the individual worker's module of desk or office, and attempts to set up a module to govern elements such as window size, spacing, and column spacing in a way that will relate to the work-station module.

The first approach gives rise to several proposals, each of which have produced its own family of executed buildings. Such attempts at establishing a standardized logic of planning have led to the plan-type involving a central core for services surrounded by floor space of a depth controlled by the anticipated penetration of light and air from the outside windows. Such a concept was dominant in the planning of the early buildings of Rockefeller Center. A refinement of this scheme leads to the lozenge shape, in which the ends of the building are stepped or tapered to create extra dimension in the portion of the building mass where the core occurs. Le Corbusier probably originated this idea. The Pirelli Building in Milan and the Pan Am Building in New York are recent examples of its use. Decreasing emphasis on the importance of windows following developments in lighting and air conditioning has tended to diminish the pertinency of this approach. The separation of the services into a tower, more or less apart from the office floor area, is another scheme with a strong appeal to the architect's desire to express internal function in external mass. It works best in buildings with small floors where distances from the core do not become excessive. Indeed, safety considerations make it impossible to use in pure form for larger floors, unless several service towers are designed with additional complexity. Square plans (such as that of the Saarinen CBS Building) are advantageous in offering space with uniform depth and access to the core and, with the core used as structure, can be free of columns up to a reasonably large size (at least 160 square feet/14.5 square meters and perhaps more). In practice, it is not clear that the claimed advantages of any one plan-type are realized with any consistency; the pressures of site limitations are, in city locations, so strong that most architects are only able to use their preferred plan-form occasionally. The attempt to establish a governing logic of modules has been, if anything, even less successful.

It is possibly because the architect's freedom is often so limited in office building design that so much attention has been lavished on the window or curtain-wall module. The eclectic skyscraper of the early 1900s had windows sized and placed to suit the architect's intentions for external appearance, usually in line with some preselected historic practice. Early cast iron loft buildings and the early Chicago school buildings, designed when there was little or no artificial light and ventilation available, exhibited maximum window area in relation to the available structural techniques. The modern architect has tended to turn back to these buildings and move ahead in the effort to find a perfect window-curtain-wall construction and form. This has led us through the era of the vertical (Daily News) versus the horizontal (McGraw Hill) exterior battle, through the expansion of window area from one-third, to one-half, and finally close to 100 percent of the external curtain wall. It is not yet clear whether 100 percent glass is too much — certainly there has been a retreat from this ideal, at least in the vertical dimension. Awareness of building orientation and the special problems of sun control is an aspect of architectural concern that grew in significance in the 1930s and 1940s, leading to such highly developed products as the well-known Ministry of Education Building in Rio de Janeiro, with its handsome system of adjustable louvers. While there is some continuing awareness of the sun and, particularly in southern climates, an occasional effort to use overhangs well, the development of special glasses that limit the penetration of sun heat and the near universal acceptance of air conditioning have made buildings more independent of this reality of site than seemed possible even 20 years ago. There still seems to be a basic absurdity in facing identical walls of windows north and south, however common this has become.

Included in the effort to find the perfect window-wall design has been the effort to find an ideal width module that must, of course, connect with the building column spacing module. There is some literature urging the virtues of various modules from 3 feet/9 meters to 8 feet/2.45 meters, but it has not become clear that any particular figure has, in practice, any special advantage, since the equipment and space needs are of nearly random variability. Where furniture and equipment (especially partitions) are to be designed to suit the building, there is certainly value in *some* module being used to coordinate these elements. But where space is to be rented to various tenants who will bring, buy, or build equipment and partitions in varied ways, the module has little consistent meaning outside of its value in easing construction and disciplining external appearance.

The 1960s brought one of the greatest booms in speculative office building construction in history. Although the architectural profession prospered in an unprecedented way, the quality of buildings produced was, in the main, indifferent. Gigantism showed up as a theme in a way that had not occurred since the 1920s and 1930s. At a time when cities were showing signs of breakdown in various systems (power, water, waste disposal, transportation, and law enforcement) the wisdom of these vast projects comes into question. In New York, the Pan American Building was certainly far above average in design quality, but its huge mass in relation to its neighbors and its location in the congested midtown area generated major criticism. The project as built has been digested into the city's matrix, but it has left doubts about whether more such projects can be absorbed.

The World Trade Center in downtown New York was planned with more concern for relationships to open space and transportation systems, but it still raises questions about the need for such vast concentrations of rentable space in a single project. In technical terms, the Trade Center is interesting for its approach to the problems of vertical transportation. The two tower buildings, higher than the Empire State Building (the previous height record holder) and with much more office space on high floors because of the absence of setbacks, would have led to an excessively large core on the lower floors to accommodate elevator shafts if elevators had been introduced in the usual way. Instead, each tower is zoned vertically into three sections that are served by a group of elevators as if the zone was a complete, smaller building. At the base of each zone is a lobby, reached, in the case of the two upper zones, by large express elevators. This division of vertical transport into express and local service gives rapid access to the high floors and conserves rentable space on the lower floors.

Another modification of the public spaces of office

(Above) The World Trade Center, New York. Photograph by the Port Authority of NY & NJ.

(Right) "Galleria" public space in the International Monetary Fund office project in Philadelphia. Vincent G. Kling & Partners, architects.

buildings has surfaced in cities where newly flexible zoning has offered encouragement; this is the introduction of major walk-through spaces at street level, usually called "gallerias" after the famous glassed over street in Milan. A galleria invites the public to pass through a building instead of skirting it on outer sidewalks and plazas. It is an extension of the concept of the underground "concourse" that surfaced in the 1930s and, like that idea, can be very successful if the location generates sufficient traffic to make the passage a lively and active space. A galleria that leads nowhere tends to become dead space, wasteful, unattractive, and even dangerous.

In Chicago, the John Hancock tower serves as that city's gesture to gigantism. The use of a diagonal, wind-bracing structure that is visible externally and the slightly inward slanting exterior walls give it an unusual appearance that has generated both praise and criticism.

In matters of detail design, Skidmore, Owings, & Merrill (SOM) has been a continuing leader. The introduction of windows set exactly flush with the other exterior surface and the combination of dark, heat-resistant glass with black surface materials has generated a "slick-surfaced," tall, black building that is much admired and imitated. Changes in zoning laws that permit towers without setbacks have been exploited in various ways, but the SOM towers, with exterior surfaces that scoop out at the base, are particularly striking.

In the end, whatever their size and whatever their exterior detail, most large office buildings have remained monotonously similar in every other way. An interesting exception is the comparatively small, tall building at 88 Pine Street in New York, designed by I. M. Pei & Partners. Although not spectacular in any way that the average passerby might note, this building is exceptional for its elegant proportions and fine detailing. Internally, the huge ribbon windows with glass, joined without interrupting mullions, make astonishing views out over the harbor available if tenants choose to exploit this possibility. This building is more than any other recent tall office "an architect's building" and is much admired in the profession.

Exceptional clients can, when they seek out exceptional architects, generate buildings that have qualities quite unusual in every way. The building designed by Kevin Roche, John Dinkeloo Associates for the Ford Foundation in New York, for example, is wrapped around two sides of a vast interior garden space, so that what would normally be an exterior wall becomes an internal membrane—an extension of the galleria idea, in a sense, to serve the entire building with a space that is not commercial but rather a spatial amenity for all the building's occupants.

The same architects' Knights of Columbus office

140 Broadway, New York. Skidmore, Owings, & Merrill, architects.

88 Pine Street, New York. I.M. Pei & Partners, architects.

Model, Knights of Colum-
bus Building, New Haven,
Connecticut. Photograph
by © Ezra Stoller
Associates.

(Below) I.B.M. World Trade
building, Pocantico Hills,
New York. Photograph by
H. Bernard Askienazy.

building in New Haven is a tower of square open floors supported by four round corner towers, which, in addition to providing the main vertical support structure, contain exit stairs and toilets. The resulting dramatic exterior form is another reminder that office buildings, when not held to the monotonous formulae dictated by the typical speculative developer, can be exciting and creative architecture.

The construction boom has, as everyone knows by now, produced a huge oversupply of office space at a time when the economy is in decline and when cities have been losing, rather than gaining, business occupancies. New York is the largest and most dramatic example, with innumerable major tower buildings standing partly empty. As a result there has been an almost complete halt in office building construction. The few exceptions to this rule are usually smaller buildings for a single tenant and are often in nonurban locations. The IBM building at Pocantico Hills designed by Edward Larabee Barnes is a good example of this type. In it, as in many such one-tenant buildings, it has been possible to plan to best accommodate the particular type of office layout (open, conventional, or combined) that the tenant company has selected. The speculative building, built with no knowledge of what the various tenants may require, must of necessity have less character and be more neutral and bland than such one-tenant projects.

The difficulty that the architect faces in the design of an office building is, in fact, that the problem is too easy. It does not involve the intricate planning and expression of many elements in the way that even a simple residence does, to say nothing of a school or hospital. The office building has more in common with the factory in its need for undifferentiated, open space with simple services in order to shelter the changing needs of equipment and worker. The architect who delights in the ingenious solution of more difficult problems is let down by a problem of such directness and is often led to tortured and over-rationalized solutions. Nevertheless, some of the best buildings of the 20th century are factories or office buildings.

Office Planning

Many jokes and much irritation among architects originate in the fact that most untrained people have no doubt of their ability to plan houses, offices, or cities. Like the man in the joke who isn't sure whether he can play the violin because he has never tried, most housewives, office workers, and certainly most executives suspect that a good plan layout is something that anyone can do who will take a few moments to try. When laymen do try to plan, however, they discover that it is an art only slightly easier than violin playing, if at all. Without special training, few people

can even draw a plan of their own home that is roughly accurate. Attempts to plan a new house lead to classic absurdities of bathrooms with no doors, kitchens remote from diningrooms, and garages too small to hold a Lambretta. The universal men of the Renaissance were often good architects and Thomas Jefferson made a fair stab at it, but most modern business executives quickly find that office planning takes a specialist.

Several volunteer specialists usually appear in office situations. One is the office manager who knows the organization better than anyone else. Another is an engineering executive (who does better than the others) who has some understanding of the language of drawings and an ability to deal with realities of physical space and function. Other volunteers may range from secretaries to high-ranking people who are frustrated interior decorators and real estate people who have a certain practical grasp of office tenancy. The fact of the matter is that all these people are invariably unable to deal with planning problems. The reason is probably based on the nature of education in the Western, 20th-century world. We learn to read, write, and to figure, but rarely do we learn to draw or model. As a result, almost everyone thinks in words, or occasionally in numbers.

We actually live and move about in space, but dealing with space is just as difficult and complex as dealing with words or numbers, and it is only the rare specialist who has had a training as intensive in two- and three-dimensional thought as the average eighth grader has had in words and figures. Mere training in spatial thinking is no guarantee of exceptional skill, but it is a first step. Training and a special skill, when combined with experience with a variety of problems, make a specialist who can take the needs expressed in words and/or figures and translate them into a workable reality. Painters and sculptors have some of these skills, but use them expressively rather than to solve practical problems. The architects are the professionals who have devoted themselves to using a vocabulary of space to solve practical problems.

Architects, however, want to build buildings. They should be able to plan the complex arrangements to go inside, but all too often they do not want to take the time or trouble. It is easier, and far more exciting, to plan a big building than to struggle with the intricate needs of one rental tenant occupying a number of floors. Most architects are willing to plan offices in buildings that they have designed, and some will work on projects in other buildings, but other specialists have, in recent years, come to dominate this field.

In Europe the "interior architect" is a well-established professional, but in America interiors have usually been seen more in terms of "decoration," meaning colors, fabrics, and fancy styles. The term "decorator" has been freely used by upholsterers, painting contractors, and furniture salesmen and has lost whatever modest meaning it ever had. The new term "interior designer," with its implication of concern going beyond the level of superficial appearance, is used by a group of increasingly prominent professionals who, in more or less cooperation with architects or architectural ideas, undertake to solve the design problems of interior space. Nevertheless, the term "interior design" carries an implication of interest in appearance rather than planning. Thus, planners (who are often also interior designers) are driven to inventing new terms to describe their functions. The term "space planner," although regarded with some suspicion by the older professionals of architecture and engineering, seems to be emerging as the favorite designation for trained experts in this field. The term suggests a limitation of scope to layout—one wonders if another expert will be needed to deal with choices of color and furniture. Ideally, one person or one team must handle both planning layout and interior design or "decoration" because these things are so closely interrelated. It is clear that the best office projects come about where there is no sharp separation of responsibility for the various aspects of the project.

A final complication has to do with the fact that office planning, as well as aspects of office organization and operation, are inseparable. Most office workers and executives sense this and will fight hard, in moving to new space, for a work situation that favors their personal ambitions and hopes. When planning is conducted as a purely abstract, spatial exercise, it can influence office performance in ways that may be surprising and perhaps undesirable. The size and location of a man's office can influence his future role in a company for good or bad. A work space can improve or degrade the performance of the people who sit in it. Decisions about equipment, furniture, and partitions influence an organization's performance in ways that are subtle, hard to trace, and sometimes unpredictable. Ideally an office should be an instrument to further the best interests of the organization occupying it. It is a rare office that makes more than a rough stab at reaching such a goal. A specialist who combines the interests of the best of space planners with skills more akin to those of a good management consultant might come closer to accomplishing what is really needed. In practice, most organizations are far too ready to assume that they know their own requirements, seeing them in terms of what is familiar and modified only by those improvements that individuals in power may demand for unclear reasons. Most planners are ready to push ahead with a plan that incorporates all the existing peculiarities and faults of the organization as it already operates.

A move to new space is an extraordinary opportunity to reevaluate an organization's structure and to improve it through the circumstances of its physical set-up. Space planning and organizational planning need to connect. The more they can be made to connect through the efforts of the client's liaison with the planner and the planner's efforts to go beyond a superficial job of layout and decoration, the more value the move to new space will have.

Many practitioners in the planning field claim to have developed a "method"—a more or less secret technique that will assure an ideal result by the application of rules or standards. An effort to search out these methods and find out what they offer has in every case led back to certain fundamentals that apply to every planning problem, from cities down to the tiniest room. The steps are always the same. They involve the discovery and definition of the problems to be solved, the proposal of tentative solutions, and the gradual refinement of a solution through successive revisions, until there is a realizable proposal sufficiently workable to be ready for construction. There follows the processing of construction in a way that will cause a minimum of trouble and cost, and a final phase of adjustment and revision to deal with whatever aspects of the problem were forgotten or misunderstood. The constructed solution finally comes as close as possible to working ideally. These steps may be aided by formal procedures, use of forms and standards, routines of work, and similar devices, but there are no mysterious secret "methods" that avoid them or take their place.

Whether the project involves the construction of a new building, a move to rented space in a new building, a move to an older building, or the reorganization of space currently occupied, each of these can modify the normal routine. The work may be done by members of an organization's own staff or by outside consultants in any conceivable combination. Basically, however, the steps will be as follows:

1. A decision (which may be tentative) to move to new office space. It is important that the reasons be defined so that the move will not turn out to be pointless. Typical reasons might be a need for more space, a desire to change location for reasons of convenience or economy, a need for offices planned to reflect an organizational change, or a desire for more efficient office conditions. A vague desire to "be up-to-date" or to modernize to keep up with competition should be suspect, because it does not generate a clear enough program to lead to good results. The desire to "be up-to-date" may be a product of real and valid requirements, but these need to be defined in specific terms.

2. Preparation of a program. In architects' terminology a "program" is a highly specific listing of require-

ments in words and figures. A good program spells out every aspect of what is needed, including intangible as well as practical requirements. The development of a successful statement of program tends to generate successful solutions. It is a truism that the adequate statement of a problem usually implies a solution. This is strikingly true of planning problems, where poor results usually spring from a program that is vague, incomplete, or inaccurate in its statement of needs. It is a natural assumption that an organization can prepare its own program of needs. In fact, unless some extraordinary situation has been established, most organizations prove to be very bad at program preparation. Differing and conflicting needs exist within any organization. Individuals can influence programming according to power and rank rather than according to validity of ideas. Status quo, habits, and routines are often accepted uncritically and built into a program without anyone's realizing that such a thing is happening. In this way, all sorts of faults are built into the new project quite unnecessarily. Most skilled planners will want to prepare the program or, at least, to study, question, and revise any program supplied by their client.

A sound program will begin with a realistic statement of the general objectives of the move to new space. It will then proceed to the following specifics:

a. A census of personnel. This means a count of bodies plus a designation of each by name, title, and function. In large organizations, individual names are not significant, except at upper ranks, and general categories will serve to define functions, but it is important that an effort be made to be as specific as possible. Connected with this census should be estimates of expansion needs (and, where appropriate, contraction possibilities) for the period that the new facility is expected to serve.

b. A census of equipment needs. This parallels the census of personnel. It is important not to make assumptions (that everyone needs a desk, for example) but instead, to search out the real needs for work surfaces, machines, storage, space, etc., for each person. Here again, in large organizations a standardized package must serve for many job classifications with study of individual needs confined to upper-level personnel.

Equipment that is not closely identified with individual workers must also be tallied in this census. This includes files, large business machines (including computers), and such items as display surfaces and conference groupings. Avoiding the word "rooms" at this point is advantageous in order to prevent making assumptions that are needlessly limiting. By fixing on equipment as the focus, com-

partmentalization due to habit can be reduced.

It is also important to assess the possibilities of new equipment that may change space requirements. This is a particularly good time to consider mechanization of routine operations, use of computers to replace manual operations, and microfiling to reduce storage requirements. The final census of equipment should show not what is now in use, but what is planned for the new situation on the basis of the best possible use of every available new device.

c. A census of other needs, real and imagined, that relate to personnel and equipment. This will include demands for space and luxury equipment associated with rank and status, needs for daylight and privacy that may be either functional or status requirements, needs for sound control around noisy equipment, special requirements for ventilation, lighting, etc. This listing of needs is most often combined uncritically with the census of people and equipment, but it is suggested here that it be isolated so that every such need may be carefully tested for its validity. Status requirements may be real, but are also often simply demands made to further the private aims of an individual or a department. It is currently fashionable to provide privacy far beyond the need of most work situations and often to the detriment of the person who has insisted on this need. The planner has an obligation to winnow out and discard as many false requirements as possible.

d. A survey of work relationships. This is vital information and central to the success of planning, but it is hard information to obtain, organize, and record. Misleading information is readily available in two forms. One is the organization chart that purports to show individual and departmental relationships. The other is the existing physical layout which, barring glaring difficulties, is supposed to be an approximation of a convenient plan. Real work relationships cutting across departmental lines are low the lines of the organizational chart, which shows lines of rank and command. Other complex relationships cutting across departmental lines are often much more vital to everyday work. Digging out the realities of these relationships and expressing them in meaningful form is very difficult. The usual tool is interviews with as many individual workers as seems practical — typical workers in the case of groups doing similar work (clerical staff, for example) — plus interviews with supervisors who are presumed to know the actual and ideal work relationships of their staffs. Such interviews increase in importance as higher organizational levels are approached and are most crucial in the case of top executives.

Information pulled out in this way is usually superior to that given by the organizational chart, but it is also subject to several limitations. People in jobs are not always accurate in their view of their work relationships. They may assume that the lines of the official chart are important and remember the daily events that follow them, while forgetting other events that are "unofficial." They may tend to emphasize events that are pleasant or that further their private goals, or situations that result from the chance of the existing set-up. Every planner who has conducted such interviews learns to recognize some of this kind of misleading data, but some will always go unrecognized.

The developers of the "office landscape" concept (which is discussed in detail later in this book) have devised a rather ingenious scheme for collecting unbiased data through a simple statistical method. They ask that every employee who will be located in a new office space be required for a period of 10 days to record the identity of every telephone contact and every personal visit made or received. The purpose and significance of the call or visit is not evaluated. The contacts are simply enumerated. These figures are then placed on a matrix chart on which every name appears (like a mileage chart on a map) and the magnitude of the figures are regarded as an index of the level of interrelationship. Groups of workers and whole departments can be treated in the same way as individuals to establish an index to the true needs for easy intercommunication.

This method, if honestly carried through, helps to uncover reality as opposed to distorted memory, wishful thinking, and deliberate misinformation. However, it also tends to uncritically record a status quo and makes no allowance for the possibility that accidents of the existing set-up may have created relationships that are, in fact, not desirable or efficient.

Until a better approach is discovered, perhaps a combination of such contact charting with interviews is the best available route to sound information on relationships. The matrix chart is probably the best available way to record this information, especially if a graphic device is used in place of figures to show the levels of relationship.

In an ideal situation, the program will stop at this point. Any further information gathered will be an unfortunate limitation on the possibility of ideal planning. Real situations are not always ideal and we must, therefore, add one more item that will appear only when circumstances make it necessary:

e. Data on available space. Ideally, this item has no meaning—that is, when space will be located or constructed to accommodate the office only *after* its planning is in progress. However, in situations where the project must be fitted into an existing space, the plan and all architectural data about the space must be included as part of the program.

The common habit of renting or building before planning the installation to be accommodated is an absurdity that every office planner faces again and again. Only a fortunate chance will make space obtained in this way turn out to be ideal. In everyday reality, the planner's job becomes one of making the best possible compromise between the ideal situation and the actualities of the space that has been preselected.

When an office must move into an existing older building for valid financial or other practical reasons, it is only reasonable to expect the planner to accept this circumstance as a proper part of the problem. However, it is still proper to question whether the space selected is in fact the best choice as compared to renting or building new space, or whether it has been chosen out of habit or out of a superficial supposition of economy.

It should be noted that the above list does *not* include a listing of floor area assignments for individuals, rooms, or departments. Such a listing is a common part of office programs, but it should not be. The decision on area assignment is a proper part of the planner's job and relates to complex matters of functional and visual planning. Needs for "generous space" or for "compactness" can be recorded under "C. A census of other needs" above, but any attempt to assign each person so many square feet will turn out to be premature, probably misleading, and often wasteful, since it can lead to building or renting an unnecessarily large area.

Of course, preliminary estimates of area needed can be made on a rule of thumb basis. Such estimates should only be made by, or in cooperation with, the planner after the general character of the space has been established, as discussed below.

3. Preliminary planning. In this step, the requirements of the program are studied and converted into spatial terms. Most planners will construct charts that may appear, at first glance, similar to the familiar organization chart. The planner's chart will use blocks sized to suggest space requirements, not to indicate the importance of the man or the unit. The arrangement of the blocks will not relate to formal organizational hierarchy but to the need for close working relationships and, therefore, to physical proximity. Such a chart can use symbols (colors, tones, visual signals) to identify needs for special quiet, light, equipment, luxury, etc., and so becomes an intermediate step between the word listings of the program and the space realities of an actual floor plan.

The same chart or additional charts can show work relationships through lines of interconnection. If the thickness of lines is made proportional to the closeness of relationship or the density of communication, an effort can be made to arrive at an arrangement of space blocks that will minimize the length of the heaviest lines. This process is a visual and graphic way of manipulating values that are otherwise very difficult to come to terms with. Such charts can establish an idea of the nature of suitable space so that when they are drawn up, before space has been selected or built, they become valuable tools for use in the next step.

4. Selection or architectural planning of new space. This step is naturally omitted where existing space is to be used. Circumstances may determine whether building or renting is best, or it may be wise to make a comparative study of these possibilities. If new building is to be undertaken, the architect's work is greatly facilitated by the preliminary planning discussed above. Under these circumstances, the probability of arriving at a practical and satisfactory building is greatly increased over the situation that arises when the architect is simply instructed to plan a certain square footage of office space.

When renting is the logical course of action, plans of available space can be compared in the light of the knowledge developed and organized in the preliminary planning phase. Spaces of the same area can vary greatly in their suitability to a given office installation. Space that commands a high rent in a top-quality building may turn out to be less suitable than less expensive space in another building because of the relationship between the actual plan shapes and the needs of a particular organization. Conversely, it may be worthwhile to pay a higher rent per foot to obtain space that, because of shape or other characteristics, can be used more efficiently than less expensive space. Sound evaluation of rental possibilities is only possible when a full program and preliminary study exist.

In both building and renting, preliminary study can clarify questions of need for window space, ideal column spacing, distribution onto one or more floors, and similar architectural questions that may otherwise be given wrong, or at best, less than optimal answers when such study has not been made.

When a new building is to be undertaken, architectural design, including basic plan and structural design, will take a substantial period of time. Thus, internal planning can proceed concurrently. Decisions about internal details, such as partitioning, lighting, surfaces, and finishes, will then be available as they are needed for incorporation into drawings and specifications.

When space is to be rented, a special complication arises because the act of renting involves the preparation and signing of a lease. Office rents are usually quoted to include provision of a standard office interior finish installation by the landlord. Just what this standard is varies from building to building and is subject to negotiation in any given building. In general, the landlord will install a rather minimal package of partitions, floor covering, ceilings, lighting, and air conditioning. Tenants requiring no more than a minimum standard may find this satisfactory, but most tenants, and particularly those interested in a high-quality office installation, will usually find that the building standard is inadequate. More and better lighting, more expensive partitions (and perhaps more of them), better floor covering and wall finishes are usually needed. How will these be provided and who will pay for them? Will credit be given for building standard items that are omitted or replaced by items that the tenant will buy? These can become very involved matters and it is the common complaint of tenants that in the confusion, the space ends up costing more than expected.

In order to avoid all confusion, it is necessary to plan, detail, and specify every aspect of the installation *before* the final negotiation of the lease. Landlord and tenant could then agree on what expenses each would meet and arrive at a rental on that basis. In practice, the cost of any detailed design when the lease is still not definite is too great a risk for the tenant to take. Having paid the cost of complete architectural and planning work, he would be so committed to the particular space that he would be at a disadvantage in negotiation. The usual compromise is to resort to a "work letter" in which the items that the landlord will provide are spelled out. This letter is then made part of the lease. It would specify exactly what kind of lighting and air conditioning, what kind and how many feet of partitioning, how many doors, and what type of floor covering in each area is to be provided in as much detail as is practical. For this to have any meaning, planning must be advanced quite far. Any departure from the work spelled out at this time tends to be excessively expensive to the tenant, since he is by then captive to the landlord and cannot seek competitive prices.

A skilled planner can aid in the preparation of a work letter that will limit later changes to a minimum, but every project will develop in ways that require some changes. An alternative arrangement that is sometimes available is to negotiate a rental on space "as is" with the tenant having the right to make interior alterations. The tenant can then obtain competitive prices from various contractors and make decisions without any involvement with the landlord. In loft buildings and some older buildings this arrangement is common. In new and better quality office buildings the landlord is usually not willing to permit many different contractors serving different tenants to work in his building. Obviously, in a new, large building where as many as fifty or sixty (or more) different tenants are simultaneously preparing space for first occupancy, chaos would result if each tenant chose a different electrician, air conditioning firm, and general contractor. The landlord must reserve the right to do this work through his own choice of contractors.

5. Final planning. Selection of rental space or architectural design of new construction establishes the exact nature of the space to be occupied. This makes possible, for the first time, the making of final planning decisions. Many of these decisions will have been made in a tentative way as part of the preliminary planning, but they can now be reviewed and fixed as:

a. Area assignments as to function, size, and location. In conventional plans this may be a matter of setting sizes and shapes of rooms, but many office areas are large and varied to a degree that steps outside the concept of a "room" as a small, box-like space.

b. Patterns of circulation and communication. These may be expressed as traffic-flow patterns, "paper-flow," or work-flow diagrams, or simply implied in the area assignments made in a floor plan. Explicit diagrams are a safer basis for evaluation.

c. Determination of other environmental factors. The presence or absence of windows and relationships of each space to public access, services, and other fixed elements is largely settled by the decisions fixed under paragraphs a and b above. Decisions about the presence of walls and partitions and their nature (solid, glass, fixed or movable, high or low), types of ceilings, floor coverings, and equipment of a built-in nature (lighting, heating, and air conditioning) are largely independent of the basic plan and need to be made at this point.

In the case of major projects, it is often worthwhile to build complete mock-up (full size model) rooms to test out the success of the planning decisions. This is a costly step, but one that can easily be justified in large jobs if it can avoid one error that will be frequently repeated, or lead to some improvements that can be incorporated in the job as actually constructed. It is most urgently necessary when the design is original and adventurous.

6. Detailing. This phase involves the selection of components to be purchased and the design of elements to be manufactured or built that will be the specific embodiment of the elements shown diagrammatically in a floor plan. In many projects innumerable detail decisions are left by default to the build-

ing landlord, contractor, or workmen. In a carefully designed job every item, down to the smallest doorknob and light switch, is selected or designed and exactly located. Many details are used in many locations and so become "typical" and a vocabulary of good "typical details" is part of the equipment of the expert designer. Such details may be used in many projects. Certain families of typical details become "systems" (ceiling systems or partition systems, for example) and can become products for industrial production. The selection of appropriate systems from the catalogs of manufacturers can solve whole ranges of detail problems, but it is important to be sure that this route is not taken out of laziness when original detail solutions might prove to be superior.

7. Selection of furniture, fabrics, colors, and finishes. This step is sometimes separated from the preceding steps and assigned to a decorator (professional or amateur), or even left to a purchasing department. Good results require a close interrelationship between architecture, planning, and "interior design" so that it is undesirable for this phase of work to be isolated in a separate department of a planning group. It should be integral with planning and detailing, conducted at the same time, and by the same people. Selections are normally made from products available, but it is always possible to design special items for custom manufacture or to make modifications in standard products where special needs warrant the trouble and cost.

It is the mark of good professional work that *all* elements that will make up a given space are brought together at one time and place for design review. Time pressures and matters of convenience make it tempting to make decisions in isolation—to select all floor coverings, for example, at one time in advance of complete design of each individual space, to standardize a choice of desk or chair, or to select a window covering without bringing all these matters together. Ideally every color and finish should be seen simultaneously in adequately large samples under lighting having the same mix as that which will be present in the finished space. Charts and schedules are the usual means of organizing this information to prepare it for the following step.

8. Specifications, contracting, and purchasing. The need for formal, written specifications arises in architectural aspects of the work where qualities and types of materials and components must be spelled out in a way that drawings cannot accomplish. Specifications for items purchased separately (furniture, textiles, carpets, light fixtures) are often not needed when the selection of specific items is made definite. If there is to be competitive bidding on such

items, tight specifications are essential in fairness both to bidders and to purchaser, to insure that all bids are on the same quality of product.

The taking of bids and letting of contracts is a specialized business procedure that lies outside the scope of this book. The manual of practice published by the American Institute of Architects (AIA) and that organization's standard forms of contracts are a sound basis for construction contract procedures. Other contracts that do not involve architectural construction can well be modeled on the AIA forms.

It is also necessary to comply with local building code regulations, which require filing of plans for approval, obtaining of building permits, and similar formalities. It is an unfortunate fact that the complexities of many building codes, combined with the bureaucratic (and frequently dishonest) operation of some city building authorities, can make this phase of work troublesome and time-consuming. It is a step that cannot be ignored, in any case.

9. Supervision. While a project is actually being executed, it is inevitable that questions will arise, errors will occur, and changes will be required. The designers concerned must remain in close touch with the work through regular visits and ready availability, if the project is not to drift far away from the original intention. Keeping complex projects on schedule is also very difficult (and often seems impossible), but good supervision and expediting can be a help.

10. Moving. The organization of a move to a new space is a vital part of the project that is often neglected. Last minute arrangements and poor planning can lead to weeks of chaos after the move. An ideal time for moving is a weekend or holiday. On the last working day, the final preparations are completed; every item is tagged and identified with a keyed plan. Skilled movers can do a huge job with great speed. If the advance planning is really complete, a business can resume on the next working day in its new location with everything in place. The organization of the move should be made the responsibility of one person, usually a member of the organization's own staff, who must have help both from the designers and planners and from his own staff. Work done in advance to make the move smooth and easy pays for itself very well in work efficiency and morale after the new space is occupied.

11. Changes and corrections. Laymen having no previous experience in large projects frequently have no notion that such a phase will be necessary, and are then shocked and upset as it develops. Actually, even small projects usually go through some phase of adjustment before they are truly finished, and in large projects this phase can stretch over years. If it is rec-

ognized in advance that this is a necessary aspect of every project, intelligent steps can be taken to prepare and to deal with the problems that are sure to arise, with a minimum of strain and bad temper.

It is also intelligent to set up machinery to deal with the continuing needs for change that any live organization must anticipate. Changes and modifications made in an unplanned, piecemeal fashion can erode a project that was originally excellent. It is a rare job that looks as well when it is 10 or 20 years old as it did when new. However, the fault is not simply in the decay of aging, but invariably in the combination of neglect and misguided modernization or change. If changes are made with the same care that went into the original design, and if routine maintenance is carefully used as a tool to improve as well as maintain, there is no reason why the quality of design should decline at all during the life of a particular project.

The outline above describes any project fairly completely as it appears to the designers and planners. It does not have much to say about the complex and often confusing relationship of the client to the project. In a small project, the client may be an individual, one person who can be talked to, asked questions, and persuaded to give answers. Most office planning projects are not done for individuals, however, but for corporations, agencies, departments, or divisions. Such clients present special difficulties to planners and often fail to arrive at the results that would serve them best for confusing reasons. The difficulties are actually not very different from problems that arise in internal organizational management. They are usually problems of communication that arise out of embarking on a major course of action without having made organizational preparations in advance. Full and accurate information must flow to the designers and planners and their proposals must have a clear channel for review and approval. In practice, the outflowing information is often vague, mistaken, and conflicting. Short-range objectives may be clear (or at least more clear), while broad major objectives are undefined or stated in words too ambiguous to guide action. Design proposals may be subject to any number of reviews having unclear and conflicting purposes. Approvals may be forthcoming only grudgingly under the pressure of time and may authorize for construction compromise schemes that are greatly inferior to earlier, clearer proposals. Every designer can tell stories of his difficulties in dealing with the eccentricities built into any number of large organizations. In general, it would seem that the greater the internal organizational health of an organization, the better are its chances of being a "good client" in the sense of offering a full and accurate program and an orderly mechanism for decision making. The reward to such a client is usually an excellent job done with a minimum of wasted time and motion—a conclusion that promotes the organization's health and leads to easy solutions to other problems. Difficulty in achieving this kind of orderly relationship with the planners is usually a symptom of management sickness and can be read as a signal of the need for change and reorganization.

There is an implication in the somewhat technical discussion of office projects above that all requirements and all solutions are a matter of simple, specific practicality. Such an approach may come close to reality in the case of a factory, where the goal of efficient production can be clearly stated. However, an office is not a factory for the production of paper. A flow of letters and forms may be one aspect of its production, but these are merely a vehicle. Its real purposes are the more complex ones discussed in our introduction: communication and control. These are human functions, not mechanical ones. Where machinery can take over parts of these office functions, machine and function together tend to move out of the significant part of the office and into factory-like machine rooms. The significant parts of the office are those where the communication is between people and where the decisions are arrived at that bring about control. Where simple efficiency is of dominating importance (let us say in a utility company's billing department), the human role is minor and machinery stands ready to take over if it has not already done so. As the office function becomes less adaptable to mechanization, as it becomes a matter of unique decision making, efficiency becomes an unclear yardstick. One slow, wise decision is clearly worth dozens of quick, efficient, foolish decisions. Communication is vital, but the matters to be communicated become complex, obscure, even intangible. This is the important vital core of the office's work. Just as the work itself becomes vitally important but intangible, so do the needs of the physical setting—the more important, the harder to define with simple precision.

This is surely the territory of greatest interest and greatest difficulty in office design. Words like "image" and "status" begin to fly as we discuss the top offices of a top corporation. The office itself becomes a device for communication; communication within the organization speaking for the roles, real or hoped-for, of the individuals and departments, as well as speaking for the character of the organization, its history and its future intentions. Equally important, or perhaps even more important, the office speaks to the outside world — to visitors, to customers, to suppliers, to competitors, to directors, and to stockholders, and finally, to the vague general public whose picture of what this organization is, or should be, has become so vital a matter of concern to every modern organization. No one will deny that a good "image" is a vital posses-

sion, but what "image" will be best for a given organization is one of the questions at the very heart of its existence. For that reason it is the kind of question least likely to have a ready or clear answer. The corporation or organization that knows what it wants in these terms is almost sure to get what it wants and needs.

The designer is, after all, a trained, professional communicator of a special type. If he is able to discover the real nature of his client's needs he has gone a long way toward finding solutions that will be successful communication. No designer can communicate intentions strongly and clearly that are vague, muddled, and contradictory. A strong designer can often impose on such a situation an ordered statement that is in fact only a statement of his design skill without relation to the organization that it houses. This is the nature of many handsome jobs that fail to satisfy their occupants. What is often not realized is that the fault may be with the occupant who could not, in fact, be satisfied by any design because his needs and intentions are unformed. Perhaps it is best when such projects drift into the hands of hacks who produce vague, muddled, and contradictory designs that are, at least, a valid expression of the organizations that ordered them. It is a common saying among designers that "clients usually get the kind of job they deserve." It does seem true that the most distinguished office buildings and office spaces tend to house the most distinguished occupants.

The Impact of Open Planning

As has already been hinted, the field of office design and planning has been rocked by the introduction of an approach so different from the norms that developed in the 1950s and early 1960s as to constitute a threatened revolution. This approach was at first known by the curious name of "office landscape," a literal translation of the term *Bürolandschaft*, the name given to it by its originators. These originators were a German firm of management consultants known as the Quickborner Team, a name derived from the place name Quickborn, a suburb of Hamburg, where the firm had its base. The Quickborner Team, under the leadership of brothers Eberhard and Wolfgang Schnelle, were primarily consultants in matters of office organization and work flow. Their interest in the physical set-up of offices was the result of an empirical discovery that the physical setting of the office affects work processes.

Their studies of this issue led to the development of a new system of office planning that produced offices strikingly different from the preexisting norms. Such offices were built and put into use first in Germany and then in other European countries. American de-

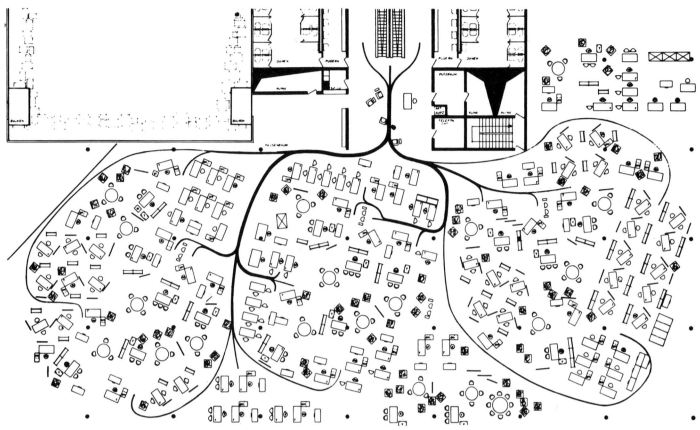

A typical landscape or open plan.

signers began to see plans published in European journals in the late 1960s that at first appeared so shocking as to suggest some sort of joke. In the typical *Bürolandschaft* plan, the entire office is a vast open space entirely without partitioning. Desks and other furniture and office equipment are distributed without any regular geometric patterning in a way that suggests that placement is totally accidental — the work of a tornado, perhaps. The first reactions of laughter were followed by curiosity, but it quickly became clear that the Quickborner Team was basing its approach on a fully developed body of theory and that the landscape offices being built were very serious efforts to deal with the problems of modern office work. The odd name, office landscape, survives as a title for this method of planning, but other terms have surfaced—such as the phrase "open planning"—to identify either the same approach or some minor variant. In any case, whether we call it "landscape" or "open plan" the idea involves the same basics. These are:

1. Planning based on a serious study of *actual* patterns of communication and work flow rather than on the formal patterns illustrated in conventional hierarchical organization charts.

2. The abandonment of fixed or semi-fixed partitioning of office space into rooms. This makes possible a new degree of flexibility so that layout can be changed quickly and inexpensively to accommodate to organizational change.

3. Abandonment of any reliance on regular orthogonal geometry as a basis for planning. Free grouping of clusters of workplaces is substituted, leading to the shocking sense of the irregularity characteristic of landscape plans.

4. With the elimination of partitioning, acoustic problems require special attention. Carpet on floors, acoustically treated ceiling systems, movable sound-absorbent screens, and often an electronically generated system of masking background sound are customary.

5. Several other less important features will be mentioned here. Although in recent years not every office landscape has incorporated all these features, they were regarded as essential by the Quickborner Team.

　　a. Insistence that open planning be applied to all of an organization, including its top executive levels.

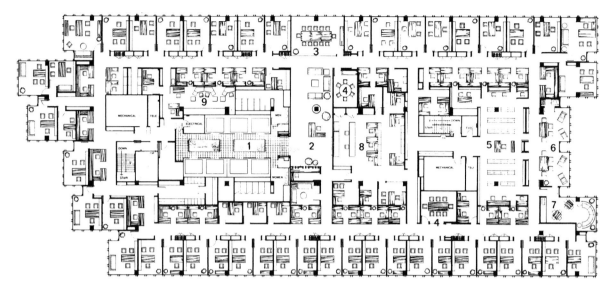

Typical conventional (partitioned) planning.

1 Elevator lobby
2 Reception
3 Board room
4 Conference room
5 Library
6 Library study
7 Lunchroom
8 Business office
9 Word processing

b. Minimization of storage at workplaces and elimination of filing distributed throughout the office in favor of a highly developed, central filing system.

c. Provision of employee lounge spaces freely available to staff for rest and coffee breaks.

d. Growing plants used extensively as secondary visual barriers and to soften the otherwise possibly forbidding character of the office space.

In what might be called "Orthodox Quickborner" planning, these principles are still respected. However, in many variants one or several of these lesser points are ignored.

The appearance of the open planning concept in the United States caused a flurry of concern on the part of professional office planners who were heavily committed to the approach that has come to be called "conventional." Architects, interior designers, and office planners who felt that their existing work was being called into question tended to oppose office landscape with considerable hostility. In fact, the most entertaining issues in the field during the last 5 or 10 years have to do with the battle between proponents of "open" and "conventional" planning. With the passage of time, the realization that the open plan idea is not totally a crackpot notion — and is here to stay in some form — has calmed down this battle among the planners. We now have a more reasonable atmosphere in which the two kinds of planning are seen as alternatives, having somewhat different merits and purposes. Office management and its planners must study each situation and decide on the best approach.

Conventional Planning Before landscape planning came along, conventional planning had become so well established that it hardly needed description. Now that it is being challenged, it is necessary to review what the more traditional approach really is. It derives from the methods of architects in dealing with many different kinds of building design and can be summarized as involving these steps:

1. The functional needs of the client that have called the project into being are listed.

2. These needs are related to space requirements in a specific way. This leads to a listing of so-called spaces or rooms that are required with the approximate square-foot areas that each will require.

3. The interrelationship of these areas is studied to determine which things need to be near each other and which can be far apart. In office planning this usually means using the typical business organization chart to identify departments and their interrelations.

4. Other requirements for the expression of hierarchical status, special desires for superior esthetic values, etc., are noted and allowed for. Top people get corner windows. Board rooms get carpet and oil paintings.

5. Circulation patterns are studied to attempt simple, direct, and linear routes of movement.

6. Planning is continued according to current architectural esthetic preferences for orderly, orthogonal geometric relationships with, possibly, occasional variations in limited introduction of curved forms or

diagonal patterns. The goal is a plan that will look clear and organized, under the assumption that this will lead to qualities of clarity and organization in the built space.

Almost all historic architecture of any merit is based on principles not very different from these; in fact, modern architecture, particularly modern architecture at its best, is usually a skillful demonstration of the application of these ideas. The best offices of the 1950s, the early 1960s, and many more recent office projects can be analyzed and admired in these terms.

Open Planning History The Schnelle brothers and their firm went about studying office realities without concern for established architectural and planning principles. Their approach is close to that of the behavioral scientists and other newly developing schools of experts concerned with the study of process in human affairs. Office work has more and more become a matter for serious study as it moves from its old role as an incidental adjunct to production into its new position as the dominant form of human work. As production becomes automated, the nature of human direction and participation becomes what we normally call "white-collar" or office activity. The management of a business or other organization controls this work and determines what it can and will accomplish. Management is an office activity too.

The study of management and the profession of "management consultant" are a natural outgrowth of this new realization that managerial issues are major human concerns—possibly one of the most important of all.

Every management consultant has some passing contact with the realities of office planning — the peculiarities of built office spaces in which status ranking, communication, and process are influenced by the fixed architectural realities of the building in which an organization lives. It remained for the Schnelles and the Quickborner Team to focus on this matter and urge some reform in current practice. The written material they developed uses as its typical case the sort of office common in Europe, and not unknown in the U.S., in which workers are placed in small rooms lined up along halls. Work relationships are only respected to the extent that room assignments follow the lines of command and responsibility illustrated in the organization chart. Actual daily communication needed for work processing does not, in most cases, follow these lines. Each person in an office organization has need for communication with others for reasons that have to do with process, not hierarchy. If studied in these terms, most office plans are absurdities.

Noting this situation on the one hand, and being aware of the new possibilities of computers as tools for processing extensive and complex data, on the other hand, the Quickborner Team proposed a new approach to planning. Every member of an organization maintains a log of *actual* communications — written, telephoned, or spoken—for a certain period of time. This data is then processed to make up a chart, or a number of charts, in which the realities of day-to-day process in the office are displayed as statistical data. Planning then proceeds as an effort to place in close proximity those who have most need to communicate. Traditionally all top executives are grouped in a status-rich executive suite. In reality, top executives often have little daily need to communicate with one another, but much need to be in contact with their own work groups. Why should a sales department or an engineering department be grouped if, in fact, its members have more need for contact with people outside their own division? This is not to suggest that such units should always be dispersed, it is merely that the real needs can only be discovered by systematic research, not by examining a preexisting chart or jumping to conclusions based on titles.

The offices planned under Quickborner Team supervision in Germany are clear demonstrations of this approach. Each worker and each group is placed entirely according to the guidance of the communication analysis; layouts are subject to constant change as the realities of the organization alter. Fixed elements are reduced to such architectural realities as stairs and toilets. In spite of the radical appearance of such offices, reports indicated that they were highly successful. The success was measured in terms of:

1. Reduced first costs for construction.

2. Low cost and great ease in making plan changes so that such changes could actually keep up with organizational needs.

3. Improved communication and work flow with the resulting improvement in overall efficiency.

4. Improvement in employee morale and job satisfaction.

Before long, offices planned on similar principles, with or without the involvement of the Quickborner Team, began to appear in other European countries — particularly in the Scandinavian countries and in England. In the United States, awareness of the concept was slow to develop and first reactions were usually skeptical. The *Interiors Second Book of Offices* included a chapter describing this approach and it appeared as an article in *Interiors* magazine. Established American office planners were inclined to attack the idea as nonsense, destined to lead to spectacular failures on first try. At about the same time, the Quickborner Team established a modest representa-

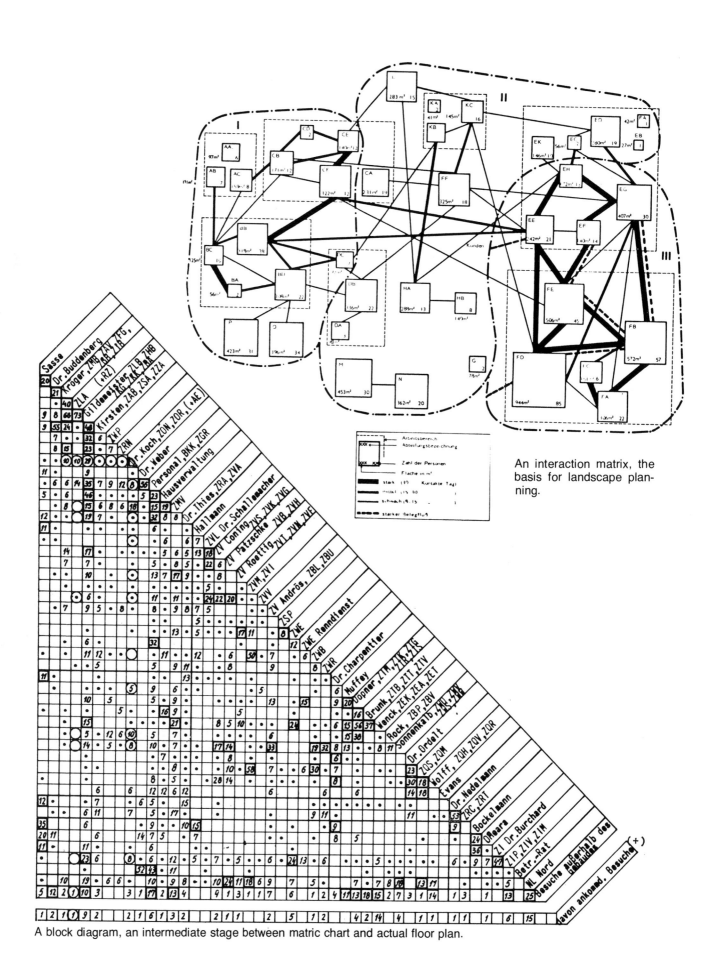

An interaction matrix, the basis for landscape planning.

A block diagram, an intermediate stage between matric chart and actual floor plan.

Landscape planning in England. Offices of Noble Lowndes Annuities in Croydon; Heal's Contract Divisions, planners. Photograph by Heal's Contracts Ltd.

tion in America and undertook to consult with the firms that showed some interest in exploring this new concept. Several companies with international extensions became aware of the European experiments (including IBM and Ford Motor Company) and experimentation in the U.S. began.

Current Practice Since the first experimentation in America in 1968–1969, the idea of landscape or open planning has become commonplace in American office design. Hardly any project of any size is undertaken without some discussion of whether this approach might be appropriate. American designers and planners have become knowledgeable about the system and are, in varying degrees, prepared to consider its use and implement it. The involvement of the Quickborner Team in projects in this country has also become quite accepted. It is one of the major concerns of the originators of the concept that wide acceptance has led to all too frequent use of the words and superficial aspects of the landscape approach without any serious effort to exploit its full potential. Such superficial landscape projects imitate the look of the original European projects without following the underlying planning principles and so may undermine acceptance of the ideas. Poor imitations that do not work cast doubt on the basics of the landscape planning approach.

A further complication has appeared as innumerable manufacturers of various office products, furniture, screens, acoustical materials, and devices have rushed to market with materials and services identified, more or less accurately, as appropriate to landscape offices.

The Quickborner theory, as applied in Germany, holds that furniture must be light and open—free of solid panels and masses. This is to avoid hard surfaces that might reflect sound and also to avoid closed storage compartments that attract the accumulation of unused stored material, which is inevitably lost and forgotten. Almost any furniture system can provide the simple tables and drawers that are considered by the Quickborner Team to be all the office furnishing that is required. In addition, open file carts and movable acoustical screens are needed. The former are also fairly common standard products, but the latter represent a new product type. Several American manufacturers have introduced groups of furniture tailored to this rather minimal set of requirements. Art Metal's group, called "TAG," and a group designed by Hans Krieks for Designcraft are good examples.

By coincidence, at the time when landscape design was first attracting attention in America, another approach to office design, which was parallel but different, was being developed by an inventor-designer named Robert Propst. Propst, with backing from Her-

man Miller, Inc. (a Michigan furniture manufacturing firm with a long history of association with quality design and innovation), was studying office work from the point of view of the individual worker and workplace. It was his conviction that standard office equipment was poorly adapted to real needs and he developed a body of theory about office work and specific furniture to serve this theory.

Propst's system was introduced by Herman Miller under the name "Action Office." Several years later it was supplanted by a similar but improved system, "Action Office II." Propst's book, *The Office—a Facility Based on Change*, presents the theoretical underpinning of this system. Like landscape planning, Action Office avoids the fixed partitions of conventional offices and substitutes movable screens. For this reason, the two systems have similarities that can lead to confusion. In practice, terminology and equipment have come to be interchanged among "landscape," "open plan," and "Action Office" to such a degree that sharp distinctions are no longer easy to make. The main distinctions are that Action Office planning provides for much more storage and varied furniture equipment and accepts the use of more enclosed spaces when and where desired. A truly orthodox office landscape is impossible to achieve with Action Office equipment alone (although certain components can be useful), and the typical Action Office installation does not conform to Quickborner policies. However, many office planners prefer to arrive at compromises between the two concepts. In any case, Propst's Action Office system has won considerable acceptance and the inevitable imitations have appeared at varying levels of price and quality.

Both approaches have moved from the stage of experiment to that of wide acceptance. The review of major projects contained in this book gives, to at least some extent, an idea of how many major corporations are in open offices. Even such traditionally conservative office users as banks and governmental agencies seem willing to use open planning in at least some situations. In fact, it is becoming easier to define the places where open plans are *not* acceptable than to characterize where they are usable. The most ardent advocates of open planning insist that there are no situations in which an open office will not work. The more usual view is that conventional planning works best where individuals work alone and separately on projects that require concentration and/or confidentiality. Probably the best example of such a situation is the kind of office in which professionals work as consultants to individual clients. Doctors in a group medical practice would be an extreme example, although it is a trifle removed from the business world. A law office is a more typical case. In fact, lawyers, when they function in other business roles, seem to form a pocket of resistance to open planning. Their training and experience requires rather studious work involving confidential matters. A private office, probably guarded by a secretary in an outer office, seems the ideal environment for this kind of work activity. Most planners will concede that the law office will probably remain conventional in plan, but what to do where lawyers show up as executives or managers in other businesses can present a problem. To provide a private office or two within an open project can be awkward in appearance and can set up implications of unintended status distinctions. To ignore the lawyers' preferences and enforce an open plan upon them can create a group of unhappy people. Provision of unassigned private spaces, studies, or "quiet rooms" to be used when there is real need for isolation is a possible compromise solution.

Another situation that tends to suggest that conventional planning may be preferable involves the office of an organization that desires to project a feeling of conservatism and dignity. Open planning *is* new and tends to look both new and lively. These usually seem desirable qualities, but there are organizations that feel differently. It is an interesting puzzle for the office planner to try to identify the *real* needs of a client organization in this respect. Organizations are made up of people and people will usually be a mix of progressivism and conservatism. Ideally, in addition to working well, an office should project a true sense of the character of the organization that occupies it. It is hard to imagine a Swiss bank embracing the concept of open planning, but when we note that the Internal Revenue Service has done so, we begin to wonder whether there are any enclaves left where it will be ruled out forever.

Equipment in Open Planning The nature of landscape or open planning simplifies most problems of office equipment. Since there are no partitions, partitions cannot present a problem. Since furniture must be movable and interchangeable, its selection must stay simple. In fact, furniture selection will usually involve selection of one system to be used throughout or, at most, two systems that are compatible and can serve to express status identification. The choice of some items — screens, files, and chairs, for example — is independent of the selection of the primary system of desks and work surfaces. The main issue raised in that primary selection is the one discussed above, that is, the choice among Action Office, its imitators, and the simpler alternative systems. The simple systems considered ideal by the Quickborner Team will usually be easier to rearrange and cheaper. But they will, in many cases, provide less storage than most American offices usually contain.

In contrast, Action Office and related systems can

An extraordinary think-tank "quiet" room at McDonald's corporation headquarters, Chicago. Designed by Associated Space Design, Inc. of Atlanta. Photograph by Balthazar Korab.

Movable screens that are a vital element of landscape office interiors. Photograph by Phokion Karas.

provide almost unlimited storage space and many special-purpose accessories, but at a price. The price is paid in money, in the acceptance of a higher level of complexity, and in a decrease in openness. This last factor arises because the components of Action Office hang from screen panels. Wherever a storage component, a work top, a shelf, or a blackboard (or any other unit) may be needed, a screen panel must be provided for support. This tends to lead to far more screening than would otherwise be necessary, and possibly more screening than is desirable. In the more orthodox approach, all furniture rests directly on the floor; screens are only introduced where they are specifically required to cut off lines of view or to provide acoustical screening.

The acoustical screens of orthodox landscape planning constitute a new furniture type. They are normally moderately curved so that they will stand up without projecting feet and so that lines of screens will form undulating patterns (or round enclosed spaces). These screens are intended to introduce additional sound-absorbing material into the office space. To be effective, the screen must be constructed to have the intended acoustical properties. This is an issue that must be checked (noting laboratory test results) when screens are being evaluated. In fact, since the areas of screens will inevitably be small, as compared with floor and ceiling, these screens cannot be expected to do more than a limited acoustical job. They cannot block off one space from another to prevent a conversation from being overheard, for example. However, they do contribute to the overall control of noise in a space, as will be discussed in detail below.

Walls are a minor factor in open plan spaces, but every space has outer perimeters. Since glass and hard surfaces are sound reflectors, it is important that walls receive some acoustical treatment. Sound-absorbing panels are available for hard surfaces and curtains and blinds have some value at windows, at least when they are drawn. Floors are invariably carpeted in every open space—the only possible exceptions being the entrance points of waiting lobbies not strictly within the working office. Hard surfaces will both create noise (sounds of feet and furniture moving about) and fail to absorb what noise there is. Carpeting both absorbs sound and tends to reduce its generation. Since the floor represents such a major area in the open office, the color, texture, and durability of the carpet chosen become important issues. Wool and various synthetic fibers are in a continuing competition, but no single fiber has proven to be clearly superior at this point. The fact that new synthetics appear constantly and are changed and (it is to be hoped) improved before extended wear experience can be developed, makes it difficult to compare them with the known qualities of wool. An interesting recent

development is called "carpet tile," carpet cut into squares and of a weave that makes the butted edges unobtrusive. The obvious advantages are that worn or damaged squares can be replaced or relocated and that access to wiring in floor systems is made easier.

The problem of wiring access remains one of the most difficult in open planning. Telephone wires and alternating current supply for typewriters and other electrical devices have normally been run in or along partitions. Without partitions, work stations stand free and can only be reached through the floor. The usual solution is a system of underfloor ducts through which wiring can pass. Outlet plates are provided in the floor where needed. Although this makes a good initial installation, it presents a problem as layout changes are made. Providing outlet plates in advance, spaced closely enough to give real flexibility, is very costly, while installing new outlets as needed is also troublesome and costly when done. I have proposed a system of slightly elevated floor plates to deal with this problem, but no manufacturer has been willing to make this product available as yet.

Another available solution, wiring through the ceiling, has had only marginal acceptance because of the appearance problems posed by the poles or flexible ducts needed to drop the wires from above.

Ceilings, usually such a neutral element in interior design, are highly important in open offices because of their role in acoustical, lighting, and ventilation systems. Although acoustical ceilings have existed for a long time, it is in the open office that their performance becomes vital. A flat ceiling of any acoustical tile or panel material can do a satisfactory job if the acoustical ratings of the material are satisfactory. More complex ceiling systems are also possible. Many early open-plan installations had specially designed ceiling systems that introduced larger areas of absorptive material than flat ceilings make possible. Some systems with deep coffers or other similar features are available as stock products. In practice it has not been necessary to use such systems, although they give better acoustical results than flat ceilings.

The ceiling is also, in almost all cases, the location for the principal lighting equipment. Daylight, available only at outside wall locations and unreliable with time and weather, is not seriously considered a significant source of light in most modern offices. The flexibility of open planning demands that a uniform light flux be available throughout the office space. Some of the more technical issues involved are discussed in a later chapter, but from the point of view of general planning, lighting requirements usually produce a regularly laid-out grid of fixtures spread throughout the office ceilings. Integration of ceiling material and lighting layout is therefore essential.

A place must also be found for air conditioning and

ventilation outlets in the ceiling. The twin systems of lighting and HVAC (heating, ventilation, and air conditioning) and their relationship is at the heart of office systems planning. The introduction of lighting fixtures that can also serve as air supply or exhaust fixtures has made this problem much simpler. Such fixtures can also offer energy and expense economies.

The final issue for discussion here has appeared as an aspect of each of the systems already discussed; that is acoustical control. The open office appears at first glance to be a potentially disastrous acoustical problem. Offices tend to be noisy, and as the noise level rises, the space becomes more irritating to its users — at an extreme level it is almost unbearable. Along with the problem of noise level, the problems of what is usually called "acoustical privacy" must be faced — that is, the matter of overhearing other conversations. Talk overheard can be a distraction and an irritation. It can also mean a loss of confidentiality, to the distress of both the ones overheard and those overhearing. In fact, this problem arises less, and is more easily dealt with, in open plans than might be expected. The secret lies in the fact that the general noise of an office — the hum of activity, phones, typewriters, conversations, and movement — generates an overall sound, a background buzz, that masks the intelligibility of conversations. This is why private conversations are quite possible in a busy restaurant. In a well-planned open office, the noise level is kept low by the presence of absorptive materials (carpeting, ceiling material, acoustical screens), while the character of the noise, its particular frequency mix, diminishes the possibility of hearing conversations at any distance. In fact, the problem most often encountered is that of too little noise — space so quiet that conversations can be heard even at a fair distance. The solution to this problem lies in introducing additional background sound artificially. The normal hiss of an air conditioning system does fairly well in this case, and some early efforts simply doctored the HVAC system to increase the sound. A wired music system is often suggested, but is far too intrusive, too subject to individual preferences, and too inconsistent to be satisfactory. The most common modern system provides a network of concealed speakers connected to a central system that generates a random background sound carefully engineered to mask conversation without being intrusive. It is a kind of sound that no one hears, but that prevents any sense of cross-interference with adjacent conversations or conferences. Technical details of such systems are also discussed in a later section.

If any systems problems remain troublesome, they are those related to the telephone. Telephone wiring has already been mentioned as a problem. Ringing, buzzing, and lights flashing each have problems —

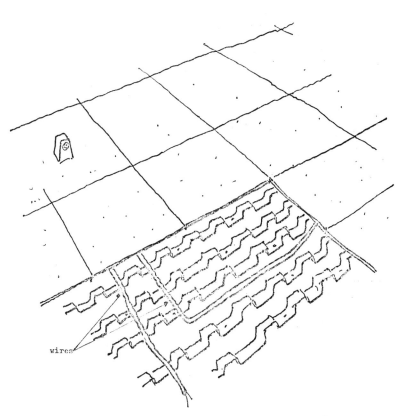

Diagram of flooring material with provision for telephone wiring; not yet an available product.

either they are too insistent or too easy to ignore. The problem of locating the person being called — who most often is not at his desk — remains unsolved. Calls interrupt conversations and meetings in progress or else lead to a cycle of call-backs that may involve many tries before communication takes place. Some of these issues are matters that reach outside the realm of office planning, but they remain problematic in every office.

Perhaps one of the main virtues of the most open of open plans is that they can reduce reliance on telephone communication — one can see where another person is and if he is engaged or free by direct vision. A gesture or a short walk to a face-to-face conversation can take the place of several calls. Sightline contact is still a highly efficient line of communication.

Does Open Planning Work? The discussions, acrimonious or otherwise, of the merits of landscape or open-plan approaches to office planning lead any reasonable person to ask some reasonable questions. Now that this way of doing things has been tried, what are the results? Do the examples we hear about and see published really turn out to have unusual merits? Are they clearly superior to conventionally planned offices that would serve the same functions?

A commonsense view suggests that answers to these questions must be readily available. What are the reactions of the people using the new offices? What about setting up an orderly test that would compare conventional planning with this new and questionable system? Isn't it possible to do a bit of research on the existing projects that will give us clear answers? Wouldn't it be possible to set up investigative research in advance of building a new project that would give a clear reading on whether or not to utilize these new concepts?

These are ideas that have occurred to innumerable planners and executives responsible for office projects. The effort to obtain readings on what has and has not been achieved, evaluations of a clear and definitive kind, has led to the appearance of a sizable number of reports, evaluations, and studies intended to settle, once and for all, the question of whether open planning really works. One would expect, with years of experience now on the books, that a devastatingly clear and sharp "yes" or "no" would emerge. However, the reality is more complex and less satisfyingly decisive. With the best of intentions, with ample resources, skilled researchers, and an output of extensive and elaborately validated statistics, there is still room for debate about the success of the open office.

If we were to attempt any sort of summary of the results of the studies that have been made, they would add up to a general conviction that there are advantages to this approach — not always the advantages that have been promised — but often advantages that are hard to pin down in statistically acceptable forms, and that accrue in places where they were not, at first, expected. It is also surprisingly hard to establish a clear framework for defining what these "advantages" are.

The efforts to make reasonable and orderly evaluations of the new open offices fit into a new concern that has surfaced in the architectural and design fields — a concern for performance evaluation. The realization that so many projects that achieve critical success do not really serve their users well has led to a desire for more solid evaluation of design performance. At the same time, the behavioral sciences have surfaced with new energy and techniques for orderly quantitative study of the performance of environments built to contain human activities. The hunger for good information coinciding with a new skill in evaluation has led to the widespread hope that we are about to develop better techniques for matching built realities to user needs. This is an area of rapidly developing explorations — an area in which, as yet, accomplishment tends to lag behind hopes.

It is in this area of developing better evaluation techniques that it seems most promising to research the success of the open office ideal. The hardheaded, "sensible person," when told of a new approach that makes great claims, asks, "How does it measure up?" What are the reports on the projects already built? Why not set up a small test and find out whether this is really such a great thing?" By now, we can survey a wide range of situations on either the basis of performance or testing, or both. There are innumerable working offices of landscape design. We can find out how they perform. Any number of "tests" have been undertaken in advance of new projects, with more or less scientific efforts being made to arrive at an evaluation of the landscape approach as compared with conventional planning.

Both the casual inquiry and the careful research approach invariably run into an unexpected difficulty. It turns out that we are really unsure what it is that we expect of an office and, therefore, the question, "Is this office better?" turns out to be an unclear question. We can get past this hurdle by establishing a set of standards for office performance (although there is no assurance that everyone will agree with the standards we choose) and by proceeding to investigate whether the open office is better by this particular set of standards. We then hit a second problem; "better" is a relative term. Asking if one office is better than another requires us to supply a norm for comparison. Is this office better than what? An old office? Some other conventional new office? An ideal office?

If this seems like quibbling and creating complexity

in a simple issue, consider a fairly typical series of events. A new office is required and the idea of open planning comes up for consideration. A committee is formed to look into the merits of the idea. The members read some accounts of the approach and look at some plans and pictures. They then disagree, some members thinking the idea absurd and others finding it very appealing. To arrive at a resolution, they decide to visit several projects and "see how well they are working out." The committee members then discover how complex the question is. The projects they visit vary quite a bit; one looks better, one looks worse (no doubt a reflection of the esthetic skill of the designer employed). The committee members may well disagree about which projects look good (since their own tastes probably vary), but they soon observe that looks are not a good test. After all, an office is intended to be a workplace, not a showplace. This leads to some interviews. Whoever is acting as a guide is asked how the office is working out. The guide usually says that it works quite well. When asked, "Is it better than your old offices?" he or she answers, "Oh yes! But our old offices were really terrible." If the committee asks how it compares with a good new office of conventional design the answers will vary. If the guide is an enthusiast, he will insist that the present plan is much better. If he is less opinionated, he may say that the conventional design could be all right too. When asked, "Does everyone like it?" the guide may say, "Well, almost everyone, at least after getting used to it." But what's the answer to the question, "Why do a few people not like it?" Here many strange answers show up. For example, A is displeased because he has had to give up his large corner office; B is unhappy because her new chair isn't comfortable; C liked the old office because it was closer to his home; while D is clearly the kind of conservative who always dislikes anything new. The issues raised here are quite typical of the negative responses one discovers, which have to do with items that either have no necessary relationship to the type of planning or are simply personal or idiosyncratic.

Why do so many people like the new office? They like it because it is new, bright, and cheerful; because it seems "progressive"; because they like plants, or any number of similar reasons that also seem incidental to the intentions of the planners. The members of the committee now tell one another that whether people "like" an office is not a very meaningful test. But what about work? Does this kind of office really turn out to be more efficient? Even this question is hard to probe. Most offices are not production units, as is the case with a factory, where work output can be measured numerically. Particularly at the higher levels of management, "production efficiency" is almost meaningless. Even such seemingly basic questions as

"Does it cost less?" or "Can more people be fitted into the same area?" are hard to answer. In terms of cost, one is confronted again with the issue of "cost less than what?" One can find out the cost per square foot of a given office, but it is almost impossible to find a comparable office, built in the same locality, at the same time, by the same contractors, but of conventional design. And even if this twin did exist, its standards of quality might be higher or lower. Frustrated by their lack of success in getting to the root of the problem, our hypothetical committee is likely to seek out systematic research reports that have been done in a number of cases to try to get a better set of answers to their questions. Several of these reports are reviewed below and the reader will discover that, in spite of the carefully planned techniques used and the statistically presented findings, the conclusions are almost as uncertain as the results of the ad hoc conversational investigations discussed above.

One last resort that has been tried in a number of cases is to build a sample office — an area of some modest size where part of the office staff can actually try out the landscape for a period of time. This has the advantage of offering an evaluation of the actual planning, materials, and equipment to be used so that it is not necessary to make allowances for these variables. It also means that the test users are actual members of the organization doing their own regular work. Such a test is, of course, subject to the so-called Hawthorne effect in which the very process of investigation generates favorable results so that it in no way guarantees against the problems of establishing criteria of excellence discussed above. If the test area is large enough, it can give fairly certain data on costs and on the merits or problems of the materials and equipment used. Where a large project is under consideration, a full-size test of this kind is usually wise. In fact, it is useful as a step in planning a conventional office too — not so much as a means of evaluating the planning approach, but as a device for "debugging" details of design and equipment.

Documentation of a number of studies and tests have been made available within the design professions over the last few years. Below is a review and discussion of five of these studies that will give the reader an idea of the techniques that have been used and the problems that are involved in eliciting clear results. If this material seems confusing and overly detailed, skip ahead to the conclusions that follow. The detail offered should be of particular interest to anyone who may be contemplating setting up a test or research project.

1. Du Pont The first office landscape in America was constructed in Wilmington, Delaware, for the Freon Division of E. I. du Pont de Nemours & Com-

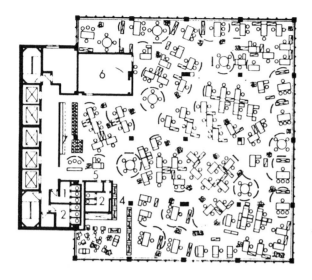

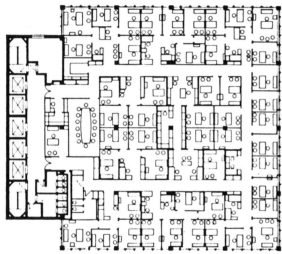

The Du Pont test space (top) compared with conventional office space in the same building (above).

A general view of the Du Pont test space.

pany. It was intended both as the permanent office facility for this group and as a general test of the concept for the benefit of all divisions of the firm as future office installations might be planned. Clarity in the test situation was, in some ways, better than usual, since the facility occupied one entire floor of a company building where other floors of conventional design existed. These provided nearly identical comparative situations. The space was put into use in September 1967 and was observed with great interest within the office design professions. Du Pont has been hospitable to innumerable visitors and has permitted publication of plans and pictures that give a good idea of the space. No specific data on test results have been released except a report that the entire 10,000 square-foot/929 square-meter area was rearranged shortly after occupancy in one weekend at a cost of only $0.36 per square foot, a startlingly low figure as compared with any similar change in conventional office space. In the absence of any formal test report, it is only possible to give some general conclusions gained in the course of a visit to the test space. It seemed clear that the space was generally well liked and worked satisfactorily. Some negative criticism had developed at first among the most senior management personnel present, the people who had formerly occupied private offices, over the "lack of privacy." In the end, two managers were located in corner positions and baffled with screens to create situations that were quite similar to closed offices. Their dissatisfaction apparently diminished either for this reason or simply through a process of acclimatization. Du Pont made no formal policy decision either for or against open planning, but their head of planning services noted that no other department had requested the use of an open plan. Whether this is because of dissatisfaction with the results of the test or because the others were not inclined to be the first to try something new, there is no way to determine.

2. PORT OF NEW YORK AUTHORITY In July 1968, a group of 41 Port Authority staff members began to use a 5,700 square-foot/530 square-meter landscape test area in the former Port Authority building in New York. Relocation of the Authority's office to the new World Trade Center was still in the future, and the test was clearly aimed at decision making for that move. Dr. Lawrence R. Zeitlin, a consultant in industrial psychology, was employed to make a systematic study of the test. His results were presented in a report entitled, "A Comparison of Employee Attitudes Toward the Conventional Office and the Landscaped Office," in April 1969.

The test area itself was planned according to the most "orthodox" Quickborner Team methods, except that density was reduced to about one person per 125 square feet/11.6 square meters, rather than the 100 square feet/9.3 square meters recommended at that time by the Quickborner Team. In fact, during the test additional people were added to the group working in the test area until by the time research was undertaken, density had reached the 100 square-foot/9.3 square-meter figure. This test area was also much visited and studied. The manager of the department occupying the space was highly enthusiastic about the concept and expressed his enthusiasm freely to all visitors. To many observers, the space looked more crowded and cluttered than might be ideal (certainly more so than the Du Pont test space), but this did not seem to present any serious problem to the occupants.

Zeitlin's research method involved developing a very complete (19-page) questionnaire using open-ended questions, multiple choice questions, and seven-step rating scales of the type:

pleasant — — — — — — —unpleasant

The questionnaire was filled out by each staff member some months before moving into the test space (to obtain reactions to the old, conventional office) and again after having worked in the test space for about 6 months. Questionnaires were mailed directly to the researcher.

The report issued includes a very full analysis of results in statistical tables, charts, and discussion. The basic finding was that the new office was well liked, particularly for its appearance and for its improved equipment (furniture, lighting, etc.). Attitudes toward work, however, were found to be virtually unchanged. The significance of these findings is diminished when we take into account that the old office was ugly and outmoded and that the test office was too small and too temporary to permit the organizational changes that Quickborner theory considers to be the main reason for open planning. Thus, the most useful research findings were that the landscape office was certainly no *worse* than the old office in any way and that it was more attractive and more pleasant than the old office.

The Port Authority test was also used as a basis for a cost comparison study. A report on this study was also made widely available; it is much more clearly favorable to the landscaped office. Space requirements are seen as reduced from an average of 160 square feet/14.5 square meters per person to 140 square feet/13 square meters per person. It has already been noted that in practice this was further reduced by crowding to 100 square feet/9.3 square meters, while still maintaining favorable attitudes to the space. Dollar cost comparisons for initial construc-

tion and changes were also given, but the figures have become obsolete with the passage of time. First costs are shown as reduced by about 60 percent, and cost of a move by about 97 percent! Although comparisons are usually favorable to the landscaped office in these areas, no other user has been able to equal these dramatic comparisons.

The absence of any strongly unfavorable findings, as well as the favorable findings on costs and employee satisfaction with appearance and amenity, led to the Port Authority's decision to use open planning for the fifteen large floors it occupies in the World Trade Center. It is interesting to note, however, that private offices were retained for "directors," the Authority's top-level managers in the new facility.

3. Eastman Kodak   In the fall of 1968, Kodak installed a test office accommodating 136 people in corporate offices at Rochester, New York. A questionnaire survey somewhat similar to those discussed above was undertaken shortly after occupancy and repeated in 1970 after enough time had elapsed to eliminate any effects of novelty. The survey and report were the work of Dr. Lane Riland and Joanne Falk of Kodak's own Personnel Relations Department. This study produced results much more strongly favorable to the landscape approach than any of the previous studies. The questionnaire used was both brief (six pages) and direct, seeking answers to such straightforward questions as:

After working in a landscape environment for over a year, how do you feel about privacy in general as compared to your previous conventional office environment?

In most cases, the questions were accompanied by a five-step rating scale for the response. In the first survey, 88 percent of the staff clearly preferred the new office; after more than a year this figure was still high: 86 percent. High scores were registered in favor of the general appearance, "atmosphere," color, and even quietness of the space. Those negative responses that were expressed reflected a feeling that the space seemed "too public." Nevertheless, a clear majority were satisfied with the level of privacy provided. Some 60 percent or more of the users also reported clear improvements in communication and working effectiveness. There was some slight difference between clerical staff and supervisory personnel, with the clerical workers more positive in their average reactions, but the difference amounted to only a few percentage points so that the test was clearly favorable to the open-plan office.

This study, and a similar one conducted in 1968 by John Hancock Mutual Life Insurance, which produced almost exactly parallel results, were so much more favorable to open planning than any previous studies

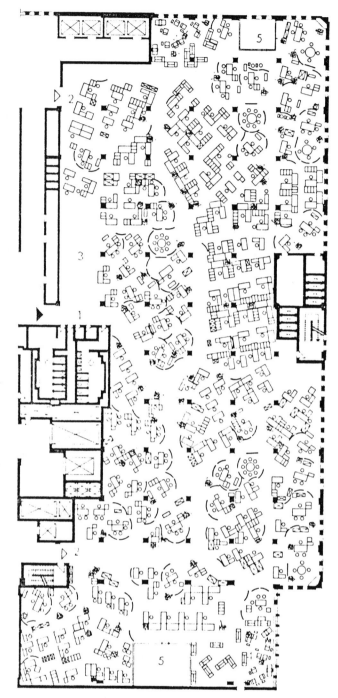

Diagram of the Eastman Kodak test space.

that they tended to cast the whole methodology of research into some doubt. No one has offered any good explanation for the widely different reactions in these various studies. The questions used in the Kodak study are, perhaps, simpler and more directly aimed at the commonsense issues of "How do you like it?" The other studies attempt to achieve a higher level of objectivity by almost concealing the purpose of the questionnaires. Asking the respondent to measure an actuality against a hypothetical ideal may avoid any tendency for the answers to be shaded to a supposition of what is wanted. At the same time this approach may tend to produce responses that are rendered inconclusive by the very remoteness of the inquiries from any immediate realities.

Another possibility advanced by some observers of these research works is that, in spite of every effort at achieving scientific objectivity, the responses are only indirectly related to the actual office environments being investigated. Users of an office may well have positive or negative feelings about the space in which they work more because of extraneous attitudes about their jobs than because of any realities of the physical environment. People who like their work, their bosses, and their company tend to have favorable reactions to everything that relates to the job. Those who have reservations, uncertainties, or even strong negative feelings about job and employer tend to project these feelings onto every circumstance of work — especially as prominent a circumstance as a new office setting. If this is the case, the results of research on the office environment are, in fact, reports on the employees' views of their jobs and employers. Although this possibility is excluded from the formal reports of test office research, informal discussions with the researchers suggest that this is, in actuality, a major consideration.

A happy staff will have a favorable reaction to almost any action the employers may take (within reason), while a resentful and critical employee group will react poorly to the very same actions that would elicit positive responses in a group with better morale. Isolation of the realities of the built space from such complexities of organizational life is difficult for researchers to achieve, and so we are still at a loss as to how to evaluate findings that are so widely varied.

4. MONTGOMERY WARD   In contrast to the Kodak study, the test and research undertaken by Montgomery Ward & Company, as reported in October 1970, produced results that were quite negative to the landscape approach. A test area of 22,000 square feet/2,046 square meters was set up to accommodate 131 employees. Investigation of results was entrusted to Malcolm Brookes of Human Factors Design and Research, Inc. Questionnaires were distributed before

A general view of the Celanese test space.

moving into the test space and after, with the by now familiar method of a five-step rating scale in which each person was asked to rate the space now in use and an ideal space. In addition, a rating was requested on the ideal space that *other* co-workers might desire. Descriptions on which ratings were requested included such terms as "aggressive," "cold," "glossy," "hostile," "meaningful," "serious," and "stable." Note that these were presented in alphabetical order. In addition, open-ended questions were asked about what seemed best and worst about the spaces in use. The complexity of this technique generated results that are not easy to interpret at a glance, but the research report included an analysis that indicated that the new office was not superior to the old in any significant way. Only a general like for the appearance of the space could be considered as clearly positive. Otherwise, the new space was evaluated as less efficient and utilitarian than the old, and problems of noise and distraction were particularly criticized.

Informal reports on this test seemed, if anything,

even more negative, with supervisory personnel especially negative, to the point of overt hostility.

In view of this test and its negative results, it is both puzzling and ironic to observe that the company's new headquarters was entirely planned and built on landscape principles and that informal reports indicate the project has been a striking success.

5. CELANESE CORPORATION While preliminary planning was in progress for the removal of the Celanese corporate headquarters to space in a new Rockefeller Center office tower, there was extended discussion of the merits of an open-plan approach. A test space was designed by office planners J. F. N. Associates and built to be ready for use in early 1971. The space was limited to only about 4,000 square feet/372 square meters for use by 13 to 20 employees. The intention was to rotate into the space groups from a number of different corporate departments. The test was to aid evaluation of landscape approaches in general, to aid department managers in deciding for

or against this approach for their own divisions of the corporation, and also to act as a laboratory for testing a new furniture system and other elements (such as lighting and background sound systems). Perhaps too much was being attempted in a short time and in a small space. In any case, the large number of variables made it difficult to isolate findings with clarity.

The space was built as simulation of the standard space in the new building. The furniture used was a new system developed by Robert Fymat of J. F. N.'s staff and built in prototype by two manufacturers, one producing the system in steel, the other in wood. The first group of test space users moved in and were generally very satisfied with the space, as was expressed in informal interviews. While this group was using the test space, it also acted as a showcase for other staff and managers who had to decide for or against an open-plan layout for their departments in the immediate future. Questionnaires were used to evaluate both the success of the planning process as well as the characteristics of the built space and its implications for organizational efficiency.

The development of the questionnaire and the evaluation and reporting of results were undertaken by Nathaniel Greenfield, a consultant to J. F. N. in behavioral psychology. The results of this investigation were generally strongly positive. Users found the test space superior to their old offices in virtually every way except in situations involving the need for privacy. While a reduction in privacy was reported, this was not evaluated as interfering with work productivity. The evaluation of the test space as a setting for work was quite favorable and evaluation of "atmosphere" and esthetic qualities, as well as the general sense of "liking," was very high.

In spite of these positive reactions, a decision was made against the use of open planning for the final project on the basis of an executive decision by the corporation's board chairman. The small size, short duration, and abortive results of this test may seem to reduce its significance, but it is a demonstration of the difficulty in translating findings into organizational decisions.

Conclusions Having turned to tests and research with the hope of finding a clear and decisive answer to the question "Is the landscape office better?" findings like those reviewed above may make you throw up your hands in despair. We are facing here the realization that testing the merits of a built environment is no simple matter. Such testing is a relatively new study— the former practice was simply to build and live with the results for better or for worse. When we consider how difficult it is to test the merits of a cold remedy or a headache cure, it should not be too surprising that testing a space used by many people for complex

purposes is not an easy methodological problem. Any researcher will agree that the questions you ask and the methods you use will influence the outcome. "Double-blind A-B tests" are hardly applicable to evaluation of an office; that is, tests in which the two samples are precisely identical in every way except for the variable being tested and in which neither the test subjects nor the test administrators know which is which. This can be done with a drug by making two pills—one real and one a placebo—but two offices inevitably reveal which is which to tester and subject. Even such techniques as establishing a parallel control group and then exchanging groups between facilities for a period of time are usually considered too time consuming and costly to be practical.

It is worthwhile to consider what research *has* found out about the open office. First of all, it is obvious that the idea is not a total failure. Pessimists on first hearing the idea have often predicted complete failure — employees quitting in numbers, breakdown of work processes, and a need to revert to conventional planning. None of these things has occurred in even the least successful tests. Note that even the Montgomery Ward test, the most negative of those reported on here, concluded only that the new office was *no better* than the conventional office. Clearly it was also no worse, and if we consider the advantages of cost, space saving, and flexibility, which did not show up in the test report, this is by no means a totally negative finding (as Ward's decision on their new headquarters suggests). The Port Authority test, somewhat more positive originally, leads to similar conclusions. Each of the other tests was essentially positive in its findings, however those findings were used.

It should also be noted that all research around questions of how well the office is *liked* run up against a difficult problem in experimental design. The questionnaire respondent, try as he may to be objective, has no way of separating his reactions to the built space from his opinions about his bosses, his work, and his company. Unhappy staff members who hate their jobs and their employers are almost certain to be negative about the office they work in. Conversely, employees with high morale who love their work and think well of their firm are highly tolerant of even poor office working conditions and are likely to feel highly favorable about any new facility. We are thus left uncertain as to whether research is really discovering reactions to the office facility or reactions to job and company. In fact, the findings are really rating a mixture of these factors, and there is no way to sort out the mix short of highly complex research involving many employers and many facilities. Such research would be far more elaborate, slow, and costly than anything that has been attempted so far and might well be threatening to organizations where negative findings about management could easily show up.

Several other points should be mentioned here. Quickborner theory has always asserted that the primary advantages of the landscape office only appear when the replanning of the office is based on organizational analysis. The aim is not merely a pretty office but one in which people are located for best performance. It is also part of the original concept that this will be most effective when applied to large groups in large spaces and when *all* members of an organization (including top-level executives) share in using open space. None of the tests can, because of their limited size and duration, test these concepts. As a result, the methods that are expected to produce the primary advantages of the approach are not being tested at all.

If there are gains in work efficiency even in these small tests, that also remains unevaluated, except insofar as it may show up in favorable estimates on the part of users. Users of an office, particularly clerical workers, are not in a position to judge the work performance of the facility in any reliable way. In fact, these are issues that are hard to evaluate at any level. Since the tests do not suggest any failings in these areas, we might guess that any impact that the open plan has in these areas would produce more favorable results than the tests suggest when the system is applied in larger areas and as intended.

It should also be noted that since the time when the tests discussed took place, various refinements to open planning have been developed. Acoustical treatment and background sound systems have been refined to reduce any problems of auditory privacy that may have been present in early installations. It has also become commonplace to include some spaces, conference rooms, or small, unassigned "quiet rooms" to provide total privacy for the few occasions when that is important (personal phone calls, sensitive negotiations, concentrated reading, or writing), with a resulting diminution in the criticism that the open office is "too public."

Of course, in the final analysis, the most significant tests are not small samples but the complete projects in which an entire organization uses open-plan space over an extended period of time. The number of such projects is now quite large and it has become increasingly clear that these projects work very well. That there are also innumerable offices of conventional plan that work well has never been in doubt. Perhaps office planners and office administrators will finally have to conclude that either approach can work well if well planned and executed. The question as to which is best must depend on what is best for a particular organization. The differences are not differences in absolute merit, but differences in *kind*. This is an issue that we are only beginning to understand.

Client Designer Project The character and success of any office design project is determined by the complex relationships among the project, the client firm or organization, and the planners or designers who carry the project through. The primary consideration in such a project must be the firm or organization that the office will serve. From the designer's point of view this is "the client." Every client is a complex of variables that represents a kind of puzzle for the designer to study and solve. How does the client organization establish its point or points of contact with the designer and how does it establish and maintain communication? These are important issues, but since they arise at the very beginning of a project, they are often ill-considered, and so haunt a project with difficulty throughout its course. The client organization in toto is usually too large, complex, and dispersed to be accessible to contact by the designer (an obvious exception is the tiny, one- to three-person organization). In some way the client must establish a temporary internal structure for the sake of the office project alone that will serve to gather sound information, supply it to the designer, evaluate design proposals, and achieve effective decision making.

There are several familiar possibilities for doing so. The first and simplest is the selection of a single person in the client organization to act as design contact and internal project manager. This person takes on great importance as the project progresses and will turn out to have considerable power, which he or she can use well or badly. The success or failure of a project can be strongly influenced by the person placed in this key position. It is a common client error to select for this role a person who is not high enough in the organizational hierarchy — an office manager or "superintendent of facilities," for example. This person often lacks authority to make decisions and make them stick and may be too accessible to political pressures within the organization. Individuals who are too highly placed, a chairman of the board or president, for example, can also prove to be poor choices because they have too many other responsibilities and therefore get distracted from concern with the project. The ideal individual will be somewhere between these levels; perhaps a vice president or a division chief who has a large enough field of view to understand all aspects of the project, has decision-making authority, and easy access to the highest levels of decision making for the resolution of differences, but also has time and energy to devote to the project. It is also important that this person have certain personality traits — traits that may seem of an almost saintly nature. The person must be patient, intelligent, inclined to cooperation rather than combat, a good maker of compromises, of course incorruptibly honest, and must have the patience and good humor to get through the irritations that every project of any size generates without developing ulcers or heart trouble.

The difficulty of finding this paragon of virtue in most organizations often leads to the formation of a committee in which the members share the burdens of project supervision. This may be a good plan or a bad one. A committee with diverse members can become a forum for warfare and a scene for decision-making deadlocks that delay a project or lead to the worst kinds of compromises that satisfy no one. However, a good committee can harmonize the complex interests of different groups (finance, personnel, maintenance, and the working groups, for example) and share the burdens of decision making.

Probably the best arrangement is a combination of these approaches; a small committee (say, three or four) with highly placed members representing the organization's broad goals—perhaps the president or division chief, a financial manager, and a personnel manager. One member of the committee is then selected to be the primary design contact and decision maker. He functions as a single contact, except for committee meetings, on a regular basis for review and, perhaps, special committee meetings to deal with highly important or difficult decisions.

Within the client organization, channels must be planned to gather accurate information about needs and to funnel these through the designer contact point into the hands of the planning group. Then, in reverse, design proposals must flow back for comment, revision, and approval. The planning organization will, in most cases, want to do some or all of the information gathering and some checking of data supplied. This is usually efficient and workable, but there must be responsible review of data as it is collected and accepted. An outside planner can easily be misled by poor data supplied from within a client organization. Poor data can come from carelessness or unfamiliarity with the planning process. It can also come from malicious efforts to influence the project for "political" reasons. Every designer has met the "empire builder" who inflates the needs of his department for space and equipment to further his own ambitions.

Assuming that the client organization has made itself ready to communicate with its designer or planner, it is time to select the person or firm (or even firms) that will fill that role. In some cases this selection may be a preexisting reality. This is often the case where a large organization has its own designer, facilities for planning, or architectural department. Even when these functions are provided "in house," the realities of the client-designer relationship apply. In fact, it is particularly important to observe good procedures if a satisfactory end product is to be achieved. Most often, an outside consultant will be

needed; this is often useful even when a project is to be done in house. The outside professional may be an architect, office planner, interior designer, or some combination of these. An architect is needed where new construction is to be undertaken. Some architects also provide planning and interior design services. In many cases it works well to start with the office planner who can study needs and develop a program before an architect is retained. In any case, selection of these professionals is very important to the smooth processing of the job and to the quality of the final results.

It is an unfortunate fact that many projects are haunted by poor relationships between client and design professionals and that friction and dissatisfaction can surface very easily during the long and complicated progress of a major project. Design and planning firms can be large or small, well known or newly founded. A very common line of action is for the client organization to make up a list of three to five possible design firms—names suggested as a result of some known project, experience of another organization, or some similar reason for nomination. Visits are then made to the firms under consideration and, possibly, to projects executed by those firms. In the end, a selection is made on the basis of whatever can be learned in this process.

There is a tendency to gravitate toward large and well-established design organizations. Certainly there is something reassuring about a well-established firm, and particularly about a record of many well-executed projects. It should still be noted that large and well-established firms sometimes leave behind unhappy clients and projects of questionable success. In the newly established firm, the individual designer will often offer more personal attention and a higher level of concern than is true of the big organization.

Recent developments have posed a new problem to the prospective client seeking office planning aid. Open planning and conventional planning have become established as such sharp alternatives as to suggest that a decision on direction must be made before selection of a planner. Certainly some firms (the Quickborner Team is the prime example) are so committed to landscape planning as to be appropriate only where this direction has already been selected. Some long-established office planners have a contrary commitment to conventional planning, although increasingly such firms seem willing to consider either direction according to the preferences of the client organization. Ideally, the planner should be willing to study the client organization and arrive at proposals using open, conventional, or both kinds of planning as the needs of the client may require. In practice, such professional detachment is rather unusual, although not impossible to find. The choice between these approaches has taken on the qualities of an ideological battle to such a degree that decision making based on rational considerations is difficult to come by.

A theoretical study of this issue done by Francis Duffy is of considerable interest here. His study was undertaken first as a Ph.D. thesis at Princeton University and has since appeared in two papers (published in *Environment and Planning B*, Vol. I, 1974). Duffy has developed a theory, and has validated it with considerable research, that suggests that open and conventional planning, as well as certain intermediate combinations of the two approaches, are appropriate to different types of organizations. If this is true, an organization can, through a kind of self-analysis, determine what approach is most appropriate to it and proceed accordingly without going through the complex tests and debates over the merits of different planning philosophies. Duffy suggests that every office organization can be analyzed in terms of two qualities, which he calls "bureaucracy" and "interaction." The level of bureaucracy (rated on a scale from low to high) describes the extent to which the organization is authoritarian, hierarchical, channeled, and rigidly organized. The military and old-line governmental departments are typically highly bureaucratic, while newly formed experimental groups, for example, are likely to be nonbureaucratic and "loose" in structure. The second quality that Duffy investigated is called "interaction," which has to do with the extent to which the members of an organization work together. Where group or team work is common and necessary the "interaction index" is high; where people work independently, it is low. A research laboratory or a law firm will usually have a low level of interaction, while an advertising group or design firm will usually have a high level of interaction. If we diagram the possible interrelationships of these two ranges of variables, we get a matrix diagram as follows:

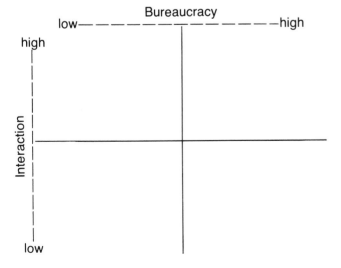

The matrix generates four possible organizational types in the four boxes. In practice, since each range of variation is a continuum, the variety of types is infinite, but the four boxes are convenient for discussion of the concept. Duffy suggests as examples of the types of organization that characterize the four boxes:

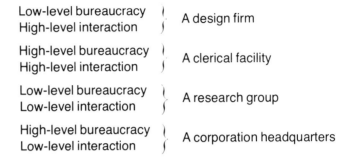

He then suggests that types of office plan be classified by two similar descriptors, which he calls "differentiation" (meaning the identification of level and status) and "subdivision" (meaning the level of physical separation or what is usually called "privacy"). This leads to a second matrix chart similar to the first but diagramming the characteristics of the built office space:

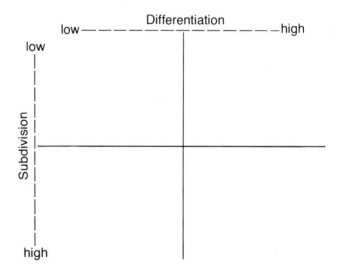

These four boxes describe the open office (low differentiation and low subdivision), the open office with private supervisory offices (low subdivision but high differentiation), the office of many similar private spaces (low differentiation and high subdivision), and the office of many, hierarchically varied spaces (high differentiation and high subdivision). It is now suggested that the two charts may be superimposed on one another to suggest the type of plan most closely related to each type of organization. Duffy's diagram makes this relationship quite clear.

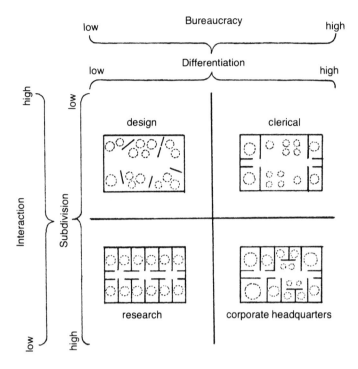

If we accept this analysis, it becomes possible to evaluate any organization in terms of these two descriptors and to plan a facility that will match the organization's needs with some confidence.

Duffy tested his theory by studying many actual organizations in their offices. He used well-developed tests to rate levels of bureaucracy and interaction, as well as levels of subdivision and differentiation. Sixteen firms were studied in this way. The planner may be inclined here to object that this study rated the existing offices occupied by each organization, ignoring the fact that this actually might not correspond to what would be ideal for the group in question. Duffy seems to have assumed that organizations will have gravitated toward physical facilities that best suit their real purposes—certainly a debatable assumption. In any case, Duffy does not find that the existing patterns conform to his chart very well. This should not surprise him since there is no evidence that existing office situations have any clear relationship to the ideal. Duffy makes the point that in reality what he calls "standing," an amalgam of training, experience, and rank, influences the individual's workplace in a way that overrides organizational characteristics. Thus subdivision and differentiation are each more influenced by the "standing" level of employees than by organizational characteristics. An organization with many highly trained, professionally qualified individuals is likely to be characterized by a high level of differentiation and subdivision, regardless of its levels of bureaucracy and interaction. Duffy does not make the point (but it should be made nevertheless) that this effect is only to be expected in a world in which com-

partmentalization has been the norm of office planning. There are, in fact, few open-plan offices, except for the clerical pools of older designs. The fact that existing reality does not conform to the proposed model does not invalidate the model as a basis for planning future projects.

In some way the client organization must come to a decision on planning approach, either before choosing a planner or, if the planner can be trusted to cooperate in either decision, in cooperation with the planner who is to carry out the project. Client organization and planner together must then develop a program of needs and requirements with sufficient clarity to serve as a basis for planning.

Plan proposals then become the responsibility of the planner, but a process of criticism and evaluation is essential to form the "feedback loop" that brings about adjustment of proposals to organizational needs through a sequence of gradually more precise plans. It is worth noting that this process of fine tuning can easily be overdone, since changes in detail requirements will be taking place on a time schedule that makes it impossible to refine every detail to perfection before putting the project in the works. Indeed, it is often best to proceed on the basis of plan proposals that are still quite general, on the theory that precise detail planning is always subject to constant change and cannot be done with any effectiveness far in advance.

However alarming it may seem to those responsible, it is often best to proceed to build space on the basis of rather rough estimates of needs. As the time of occupancy grows closer, more detailed planning can be undertaken, with final adjustment to immediate needs left to the very moment of occupancy. This runs counter to most people's sense of the proper way to proceed, but it can be far more efficient than planning down to the last detail far in advance. This usually leads to a long series of troublesome revisions during the process of construction to take into account the inevitable changes in organizational realities that will occur during the long period (6 months to 2 years) between the time when work is begun and the time of actual occupancy.

The appropriate amount of participation on the part of the projected users of an office space in the planning process remains a matter for discussion. Traditionally, users had no role. They were represented by their chiefs who simply directed what was to be provided. This way of proceeding leads to a "put up or shut up" relationship between project manager and user that has potentialities for stress. The Quickborner Team has been particularly vocal in urging that users should have a major role in the planning process. Since there are many users, most are often lacking in any planning skills or grasp of overall organizational needs, and may well have a transitory relationship to their working roles. Thus, providing them with a significant role in planning is not always easy. One approach often used is to offer to projected user groups some exposure to projected plans—perhaps best presented in the form of scale models—for comment and possible revision. Suggestions of value may surface, and even if they do not, the step is often useful in giving to the projected users some sense of involvement in the planning process.

Modern office planning tends to break into two phases that have some interrelationships, but also have a high degree of independence. One aspect is planning in the literal sense—the development of layouts as set forth in floor plans. The second aspect is the choice of systems and equipment. As these two factors pull together in the execution of the project, they establish its final character in both concept and detail. It is possible to select systems of floor and ceiling construction, lighting, acoustical control, and furniture in advance of planning. It is also possible to plan before these system selections have been made. Normal common-sense ways of working tend to place planning first and system selections second. Yet, in reality, the reverse order is probably better. Systems, particularly furniture systems, influence what can be done in planning terms, at least at the detail level. This suggests that the most logical way to proceed is the rather unexpected one of *first* choosing lighting, furniture, and other systems to be used and only afterwards proceeding to planning. Estimates of space requirements and general assignments of space can,

of course, come first. This is particularly urgent in multifloor projects and where questions of space rental or space construction must be dealt with well in advance of detailed planning. Thus the following sequence emerges as desirable:

1. Survey of requirements and development of program.

2. Establishment of space needs in terms of areas and, in multifloor projects, "stacking" or assignment of space to floors.

3. Study of more detailed space requirements and relationships. Establish areas and adjacency requirements by individual workplace with estimates of expansion needs.

4. Selection of systems and equipment.

5. Detailed final planning with the expectation of one or more cycles of revision to adjust to detailed needs.

6. Contracting and ordering to get the project started.

The key decisions that determine the quality and character of a project are, of course, concealed in such a simple outline of the steps to be taken. They are made when organizational management first characterizes its needs and, probably most important of all, when a selection of designer/planner is made. The other steps are more routine; but it is these major decisions that will determine the success of the project as built.

CASE STUDIES

In this section, a number of office planning projects are illustrated as totalities. The choice of projects was inevitably difficult and no doubt, in the end, somewhat arbitrary. All projects selected are large enough to illustrate a variety of spaces and problems. Variety of approach has also been sought. Conventional planning and open planning in several forms are represented, as are offices in new buildings and old, in rented and owned space, in city and in exurban locations.

It is an embarrassment in any selection of this kind to find that certain names of architects and designers occur again and again. The best work comes from the best firms and the number of the best firms is always limited. In the end, eighteen organizations are represented in these twelve projects so that the repetitions are not excessive—especially since firms that appear more than once appear in every case as part of different collaborations. Of course, it is unfortunately true that availability of information and illustrations is a factor in selection. If there are even more interesting projects that were omitted here because they were unknown to the writer, perhaps they will surface in time for an *Interiors 4th Book of Offices*.

MGIC Plaza

Milwaukee, Wisconsin
Skidmore, Owings, & Merrill (Chicago), architects and engineers
Warren Platner Associates, interior designers

This insurance company headquarters was conceived with the architectural dignity of a civic monument. It consists of two related buildings standing in an ordered relationship on a podium-like platform. The larger "investment" office building is a simple block mass housing general offices. It acts as a backdrop for the smaller but more spectacular "headquarters" building, which houses executive offices. A bridge connects the two at the second-floor level, while the base platform makes a stronger visual tie.

Each building uses a structural grid of columns on a uniform 30-foot/9-meter spacing. Externally, the columns are not visible in the office block, although their spacing can be felt in the window grid—three windows to a bay. In contrast, the headquarters block displays the column cage spectacularly. Its top (fourth) floor cantilevers out from the outermost columns, while below, the third, second, and first floors become successively smaller, permitting the columns to emerge externally—an inverted, stepped pyramid held up by exposed columns. Platner's approach to the interior design is the antithesis of the total flexibility concept reflected in so many other recent projects. Instead, here everything seems permanent (even partitions that are actually movable), dignified, and monumental. Materials and colors have great consistency throughout the building. The emphasis is not on

Typical private office in MGIC headquarters building. All photographs of MGIC Plaza by Ezra Stoller © ESTO.

variety or contrast but on coherence and continuity. The columns within the building are wrapped in the same travertine facing used outside, and every column is visible—often in two or more adjacent rooms. Brown wool carpeting is used everywhere, with a border of ivory vinyl outlining the shape of each space. Other materials stay close to the color range of travertine, carpet, and bronze. Sculptured textile tapestries by Sheila Hicks appear in key locations in a color range close to ivory and gold. The Alicia Penabba sculpture is of bronze. All the furniture is of Platner's own design for various manufacturers, some of it developed especially for this building.

Except for special purposes and accent lights in a few locations, lighting is consistent throughout the building. Square fluorescent fixtures are fitted into the square grid of the concrete structure. The warmth of the color and materials used are planned to counter and relieve any sense of coldness that may derive from the uniform and cool lighting.

This project, probably more than any other described in this book, exemplifies a design direction that accepts the idea that a corporate office can be a monument with the classic monumental attributes of dignity and permanence. Monumentality always carries with it the danger of pomposity and implications of authoritarianism. In this building (as in his well-known earlier project for the Ford Foundation in New York), Plattner has tried to counter any such unfortunate implications by minimizing hierarchical distinctions through consistent use of materials and details in executive and work areas alike and by relieving any sense of forbidding sternness through the use of warm colors and sympathetic materials. The sense of richness and grandeur is certainly present, but it is present throughout, not just in an exclusive executive suite. As a young company growing rapidly in a field where stability is vital, MGIC was clearly seeking a tangible expression for its own sense of corporate self. To express this sense through the media of architecture and art in the creation of a modern monumentality is as much a contribution to the modern city as were the parks and palaces that give character to so many European cities.

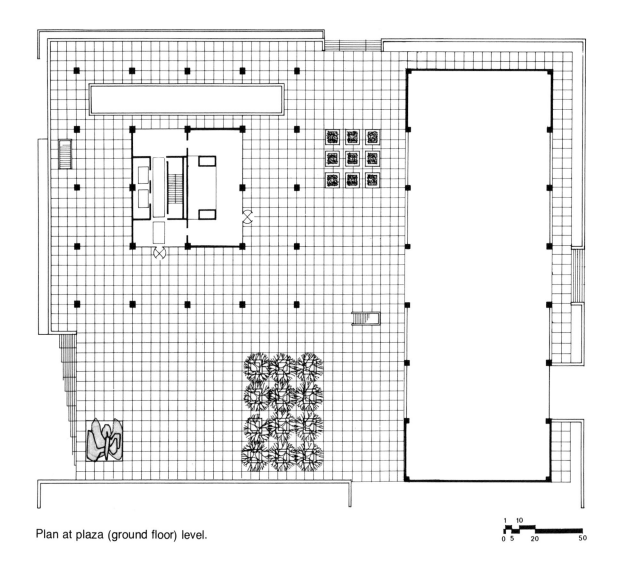

Plan at plaza (ground floor) level.

Reception area with Platner-designed standard furniture.

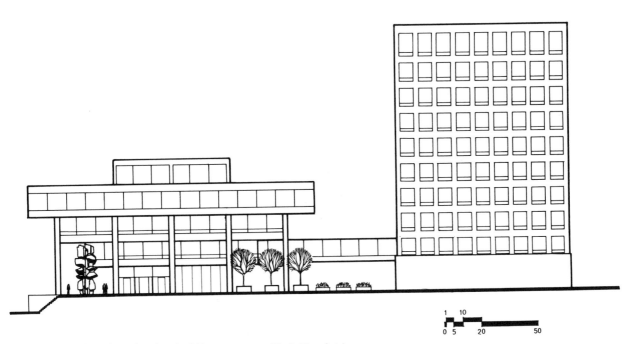

Diagrammatic elevation showing building masses with linking bridge.

(Right) Plan of fourth (and largest) floor of the headquarters building.

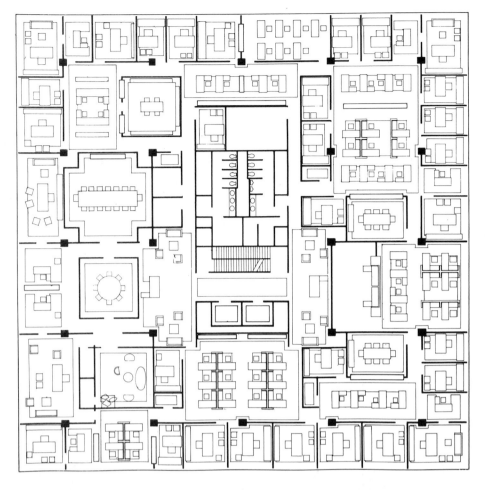

(Below) Secretarial space with integrated partition, ceiling, and storage systems.

Typical office work station group.

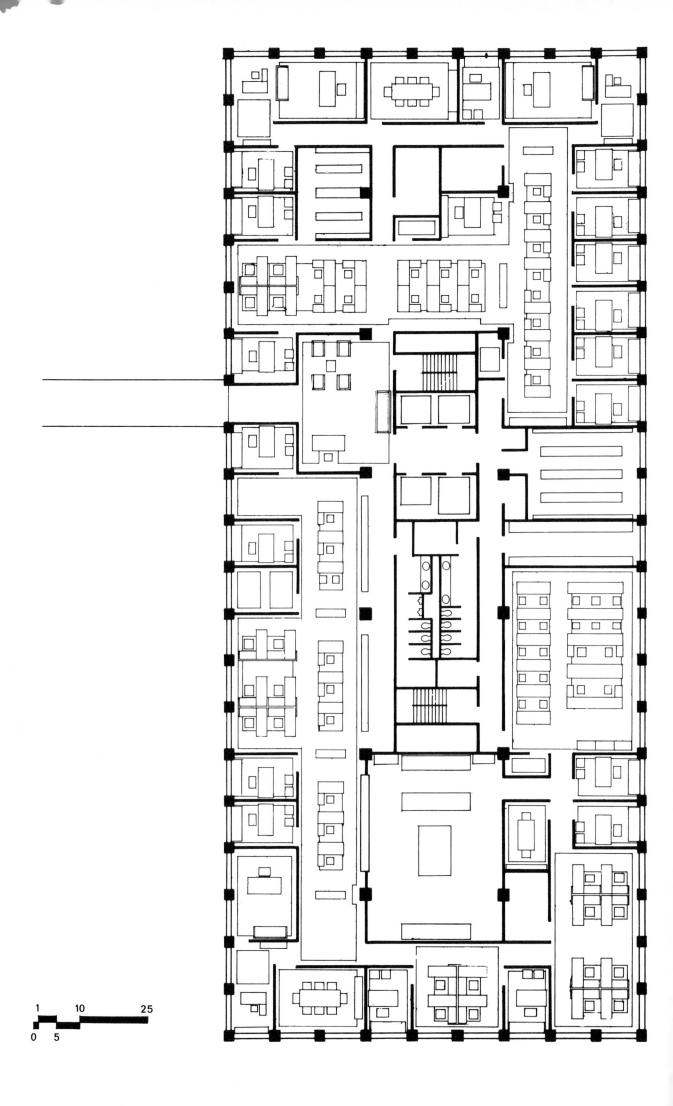

1   10   25
0   5

(Left) One of two employees' dining rooms.

(Opposite page) Typical floor plan in investment building.

(Below) Executive office.

Charles J. Havelka

Sears Tower

Sears, Roebuck and Company Headquarters
Chicago, Illinois
Skidmore, Owings, & Merrill, architects
SLS/Environetics, Inc., space planners and interior designers

If for no other reason, the sheer size of this project would mark it as one of the key office installations of the 1970s. The building is the tallest and largest commercial office structure yet built — 110 stories, 1,454 feet/436 meters high. The floor area enclosed amounts to some 4.5 million square feet/418,500 square meters. Of this, Sears occupies 2.2 million square feet/204,600 square meters on the lower fifty floors to house some 7,000 employees.

SLS devoted years to the preliminary study of space requirements, work relationships, and existing equipment that might be reused. (In the end nothing was reused.) If any project could justify the need to use computer aids to manage the massive quantity of data, this project would surely qualify. In fact, computer data handling became a key element in the organization and processing of the project. The current and future needs of ninety-three departments were analyzed and dealt with, both in terms of blocks of space and space locations, and in terms of individual requirements for space and equipment for each individual person. Certainly human memory and such traditional aids as notes on a yellow pad could not possibly have been adequate to handle such masses of information.

The building developed by Skidmore, Owings, & Merrill (SOM) is an austere geometric block organized in plan as a square made up of a 3 x 3 arrangement of lesser squares. As the mass of the building rises, certain of the subsquares drop out until only two survive to the topmost floors. Each of the internal subsquares measures 75 square feet/6.96 square meters and is column-free. SLS referred to these squares as "megamodules."

The interior planning can be described as conventional in that it is not based on any particular planning doctrine. Private offices, semiprivate offices, departmental spaces enclosed by partitions, and open work areas are all used as requirements may suggest. Layout is generally geometric and there is great reliance on standardization throughout the project. Most floors are, in the main, assemblies of standardized office and work station types. Each floor is divided into quadrants, four areas formed by diagonal division of the plan square for color specification. Five basic color schemes were established, each using a range of analogous colors and each sharing certain colors in the color wheel with the adjacent scheme. These schemes are then used in sequence in the adjacent quadrants of a floor and shift into the next adjacent schemes on the next floors above and below. It is a system that gives rise to constant variation in color while maintaining coherent relationships to avoid any sense of either monotony or chaos. Color assignments are also used functionally to establish departmental identification through color keying to help visitors (and employees) avoid the hazard of getting lost in the vast expanses of complex spaces.

Of course, standard office spaces are varied because of the need for conference and meeting rooms, training rooms, board rooms, and similar special-purpose facilities. For example, the twenty-seventh floor is entirely devoted to audio-visual facilities, including a complete TV studio.

SLS has been a highly vocal proponent of computer aids for space-planning work and this project was an ideal laboratory for demonstrating the usefulness of such methods. Under the name "Man/Mac" (for man-machine), SLS has developed a computer-based system for storing information and producing drawings. Rough sketches can be fed to input devices, modified by light-pen on a scope, stored on tape, and then converted to drafted plans entirely automatically. This way of dealing with such a vast project made it possible to process endless revisions, maintain accurate records, and generate needed drawings and specifications with a minimum of costly handwork and a minimum of human error.

At least at the present stage of computer technique, working in this way requires a willingness to stay with highly organized standards and deal in relatively simple geometric relationships. Since these were the desires of SOM and SLS in any case, and since the project's magnitude almost required such an orderly approach, computer techniques seem to have been ideally adapted to this project. Although it may be a slight exaggeration, we might almost describe the Sears Tower offices as the first full-fledged example of computer-aided office design.

Typical 10 × 15 feet/3 × 4.6 meter private office. All photographs of Sears Tower by Louis Reens.

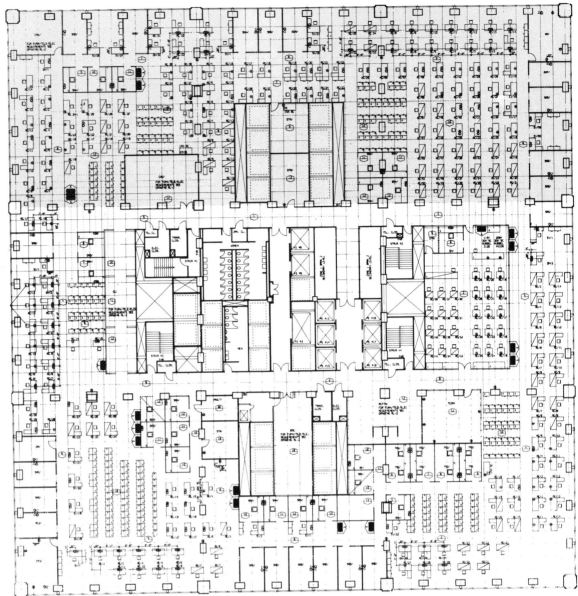

(Right) A typical floor plan below the 50th floor (where setbacks begin). Gray tone identifies three of nine mega-modules.

(Below) Reception areas are generally similar but are identified by varying color. A standard graphic system is used throughout.

(Left) Semiprivate offices 10 x 10 feet/3 x 3 meter are separated by 62-inch/ 1580-millimeter partitions that support work counters and storage units.

(Below) Flexible meeting room.

Reception area for the medical department, typical of reception, lounge, and waiting areas. Color in this case is red, orange, and yellow with a predominantly red wall hanging.

The board room with horseshoe table and the traditional ceremonial portraits.

Volvo of America Corporation Headquarters

Rockleigh, New Jersey
Goldstone, Dearborn, & Hinz, architects and interior designers

This suburban office building is an excellent example of the way in which office landscape concepts have been assimilated into American office design practice. The building is a simple two-story rectangle with a projecting square block forming a T shape. The ground floor is largely devoted to services, files, computer room, mail and shipping rooms. An employees' diningroom and lounge open on to an adjacent terrace. The public entrance to the building is in the center of the west side, while the employees' entrance is in the projecting block on the east. An auditorium seating 100 with a platform stage and full projection facilities is on the ground floor adjacent to the entrance. On the upper level the projecting block contains a lounge and three conference rooms with folding partition dividers. This block is a solid mass with only minimal window space. The main rectangular block, 100 by 215 feet/30 by 64.5 meters, is, on the upper level, entirely glazed on all four sides with gray, heat-resistant glass. A stairway from the public lobby gives access through an open well. The space is completely open and columnless, permitting a totally flexible open-plan office floor. At the time when the occupants moved in, about 100 people were accommodated, but the space is planned to be adequate for expansion needs up to about a total of 200.

A 5-foot/1.5-meter modular grid relating to the perimeter glass division is visible in the integrated ceiling system, which incorporates lighting, acoustical treatment, air conditioning, and sprinklers in a unified pattern. Floor outlets for AC and telephone are provided, less visibly, in a staggered 5-foot grid. The floor covering is a 1-square-foot/0.09-square-meter carpet tile laid loose so that access to floor services is easy. The layout of the general office space is an example of a middle ground between orthodox landscape and conventional planning. Most of the space is open and divided only by movable screens and other furniture units. However, the layout is geometric and maintains patterns of relationship of an architectural kind rather than using the more random scramble characteristic of *Bürolandschaft*. There are also fully enclosed and fully private offices for two top men. Although created from movable units that do not extend to the ceiling, there are also other management offices clustered at the corners of the building in a way that clearly denotes status through the familiar and conventional symbolism.

From the point of view of the originators of landscape planning, such a project may hardly seem to qualify as being an example of that approach at all. From the point of view of the office worker accustomed to offices as a complex of small spaces defined by innumerable partitions and doors, this open approach seems new and radical.

Published reports of users' comments after the building had been in use for some time indicate a generally high level of satisfaction. The excellent appearance of the main work space seems to be universally admired. The feared problems of noise and inadequate privacy have not materialized. It might be noted, however, that since occupancy is only at about 50 percent of planned capacity, these issues have not yet been put to a very stringent test. The many small conference rooms scattered through the work space are appreciated both for meetings and as retreats for use when special privacy is needed. Mildly critical comments also seem to have surfaced about the clearly visible preservation of status indication through stepped levels of increasing privacy. No one seems to suggest that this is objectionable in any functional way. It is rather that the promise of total democracy that open planning seems to hold out may make the realities of corporate hierarchy *more* visible than they are in conventional planning, where these facts of life are so extensive that they have come to be accepted as normal and inevitable.

The dining terrace seen from the upper floor. All photographs of Volvo by Bill Rothschild.

Plan of main office floor.

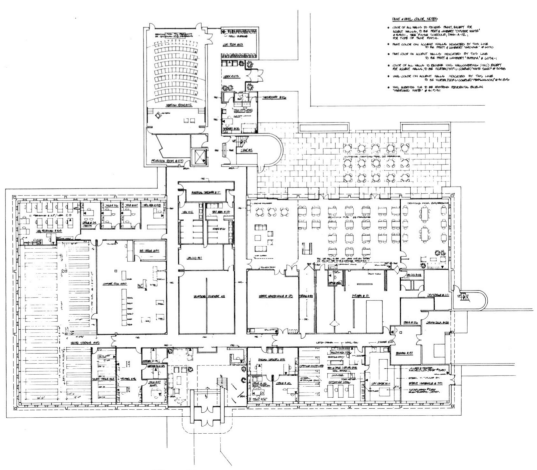

Plan of lower (ground) floor.

(Above) Public reception
area on lower floor. Stair
rises in well that connects
to main office area.

(Left) The open office
space becomes visible
from the stair landing.

The main office area, more open here than it will be when building utilization increases to full occupancy.

Employees' dining room. Door out of sight on the left opens onto an adjacent terrace.

Lounge on the upper floor.

Auditorium–meeting room on the lower floor.

General view of Boston City Hall.

Boston City Hall

Boston, Massachusetts
Kallmann, McKinnell, & Knowles, architects
Becker & Becker Associates, Inc., space planners
I.S.D., Inc., interior designers
Ann Sullivan, Tom Rowlands, interior designers for the mayor's suite

Perhaps it is debatable whether a city hall is, in fact, an office building and therefore eligible to appear in this book. While this city hall is — as might be expected of such a building in any major city — a ceremonial monument, it is also an office building insofar as its major function is concerned. That it is so different from the typical corporate office and at the same time of such exceptional excellence makes it appropriate for some special study here.

The origins of the building's architecture are in themselves exceptional. Competition as a device for selecting architects has fallen into disuse, for reasons that are not too clear. The competitions of the 1920s and 1930s generated some highly successful projects, all too often never built (for example, the Saarinen-Swanson design for the Smithsonian Gallery for Washington, D.C.), as well as some rather painful controversies. The almost standard use of competition to select architects for major projects in Finland is often credited as a factor in the surprisingly high quality of architectural production in that tiny country. In the United States, selection by competition has been a rarity in recent years. In this instance, however, with a carefully prepared program developed from Becker & Becker's research, a competition brought the commission for this major building to a young partnership that would almost surely never have been in the running under any other circumstances. The resulting building is a striking exception to the normal dullness and routine of most governmentally sponsored construction. The striking exterior form and dramatic public spaces are not the major concern of this book. However, the largest part of the building is—as is the case with most public buildings — a series of office floors.

Instead of allocating the minimum budget to build the standard interiors that one thinks of as "civil service" design, the city allowed enough money for this building to have interior spaces of high quality and great originality. The quality of the working spaces has great integrity—the thin and synthetic sense of so much speculative office building interior design is replaced by a solidity and directness that is quite special. The sturdy, austere, and "brutalist" quality of the architecture shows through everywhere and is supported rather than countered in the simple and direct selection of furniture and finishes. Style is not much in evidence—there is no sense of design for the current moment. Instead, the interiors share the slightly solemn, very monumental, and basically serious character of the building itself.

In the case of the mayor's office suite, Mayor Kevin White chose to engage Ann Sullivan and Tom Rowlands to develop a special approach to the space involved. By good fortune, these designers did not elect to try for contrast by approaching their assignment in a way totally different from the balance of the building. The mayor's suite is somewhat more special, somewhat more luxurious, somewhat more personal in character, but the character still shares the basic dignity and monumentality of the building and fits in with the overall design by I.S.D. so well as to take its place as an integral part of the total project.

This is an architecturally complex building with major public spaces laced into lower levels through the fourth floor. The fifth floor is the special, ceremonial office level with the mayor's suite, the council chamber, and councilmen's offices. The three levels above make up, for all practical purposes, an office building in the form of a large rectangle around a central court. On these levels, which are the homes of the city's bureaucracies, the building's powerfully unique structural system dominates in the character of the overhead structure with its integral lighting. The simplicity and quiet color of the various counters, files, desks, and partitions remain subservient to the dominating character of the building. One is always aware that this is City Hall, a very exceptional place, not a routine office building of the sort that any transient commercial tenant might occupy.

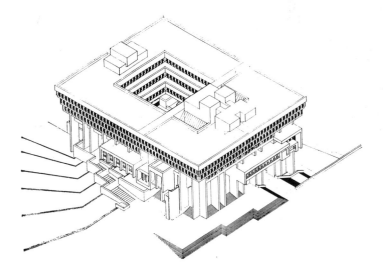

Isometric line drawing.

South lobby, the main public and ceremonial entrance space.

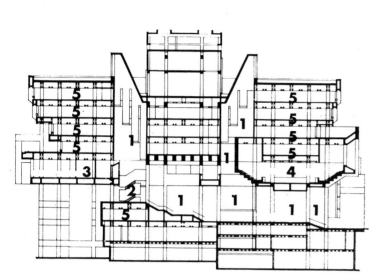

East-West Section Thru Council Chamber and South Lobby
1 south lobby and its skylit shafts
2 mayor's stair
3 mayor's offices
4 council chamber
5 city offices

East-west section.

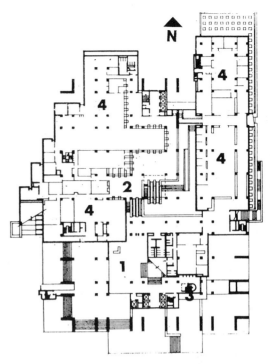

Third Floor Plan
1 south lobby
2 open courtyard
3 mayor's stair
4 offices

Plan of third floor (south lobby) level.

Eighth Floor
1 open court and terrace
2 public corridors, empty space
3 service
4 offices and conference rooms,
   including Workmen's Compen-
   sation, Redevelopment Authority, Real Property, Parks
   & Recreation, etc. etc.
5 Building Department
6 Cashier
7 Public Service Counters
8 Building Department
   Administration

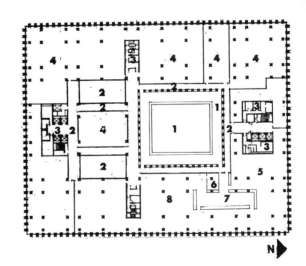

Eighth floor plan, the topmost office level.

(Left, top) A typical department head's office. Photograph by Ezra Stoller © ESTO.

(Above) Office of the board chairman, assessing department. Photograph by Ezra Stoller © ESTO.

(Bottom) Work space in the building department. Photograph by Olga Gueft.

The mayor's reception room. Photograph by Alexandre Georges.

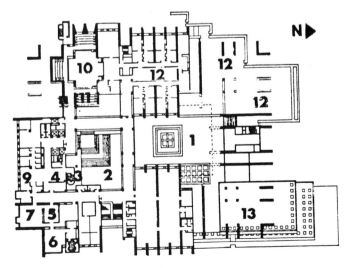

N▶

Fifth Floor
1 open court
2 south lobby
3 mayor's stair
4 reception of mayor's
  department
5 reception of mayor's
  personal office
6 mayor's conference room
7 mayor's private office
8 mayor's dressing room
  and bath
9 offices of mayor's staff
10 council chamber
11 council chamber galleries
  and access
12 councilors' offices
  and conference rooms
13 exhibition hall

Plan of the fifth floor with mayor's suite.

(Right) Mayor's office. Photograph by Olga Gueft.

Two views of mayor's conference room. Photographs by Olga Gueft.

IBM World Trade Americas/Far East Corporation Headquarters

Mount Pleasant, New York
Edward Larrabee Barnes Associates, architects and interior designers

This building occupies land that was originally part of the Rockefeller family Pocantico Hills estate. A key requirement for architectural design was that the building should cause only a minimal disruption of the natural beauty of the site. The building as built is in the form of a giant W, built into the hillside so that it is two stories high on one side and three stories on the other. The employee entrance on the uphill side is at the second level so that a maximum of one flight of stairs gives access to every part of the building. The building exterior of glass and smooth metal is highly reflective. The surrounding moat of water sets up a series of reflections that help to tie the structure into the site and minimize its mass. In the parking areas, clusters of trees are preserved to give as much of a wooded character as possible.

The lower floor, built back into the hillside on the parking lot side, is largely devoted to services, a computer area and some related offices, and, on the central axis, an employees' cafeteria. The second or middle level provides public access at the center point and employee entrances at the bends of the W on right and left sides. This level, as well as the third and topmost level above, are largely open space devoted to open offices. Conference rooms, lounges, and the few private offices required are strung out along the rear edge (toward the hillside). The major line of circulation follows along the building perimeter, with the complex interactions of outside view and glass reflections forming a visual screen at the outside wall. Inside, patterns are formed by the massing of movable screens, white blocks of Modulo II office furniture, and plants. Lighting is in linear bands of fluorescent strips in the ceiling roughly parallel to the W form of the building. Open stairs connect the levels and lead directly to the cafeteria on the lower level.

While the quiet color and ribbon glass of the exterior makes the building relatively unobtrusive in the landscape, the same ribbon glass makes the out-of-doors a strong influence internally. Vistas across the working spaces are not stopped by the windows, but rather flow outside so that a background of sky and trees seems to be accessible almost everywhere. Since circulation follows the outer walls, all work spaces have approximately equal access to the view — no one has his own window; everyone feels in touch with the light and air. (A few top executive offices that are conventionally partitioned are the only exceptions to this pattern.)

Office supply distribution, mail, and interoffice paper distribution and copy services are integrated into a system using conveyors concealed above the ceilings connecting central stations on each floor. As one might expect of an IBM facility, there is full use of computer-based data handling and communication systems. Building security is established through the use of magnetically coded badges that unlock doors only as programmed coding permits.

The role that corporate art occupies in so many company headquarters, as well as the role of focal points and visual distractions, is conceived of here in a somewhat different way than usual. The graphic designers Chermayeff & Geismer have assembled a number of collections of everyday small objects from all over the world and carefully arranged them in displays of "things," tightly packed into plastic boxes. For example, in the main entrance lobby there is a display of some 82,000 postage stamps arranged in 360 Lucite boxes stretching for a width of 30 feet/9 meters.

This project seems to suggest a delicate balance between the pride and grandeur of the corporate identity as quasiroyal patron of greatness in design and another, newer role for the corporation as modest, discreet patron of the design arts and steward of things and places. The desire to conserve, to maintain existing landscape, and to be a good employer and a good neighbor are as important in this project as are any of the qualities of pride and display.

The main public reception area with a skylight over the curved seating unit. Photograph by H. Bernard Askienazy.

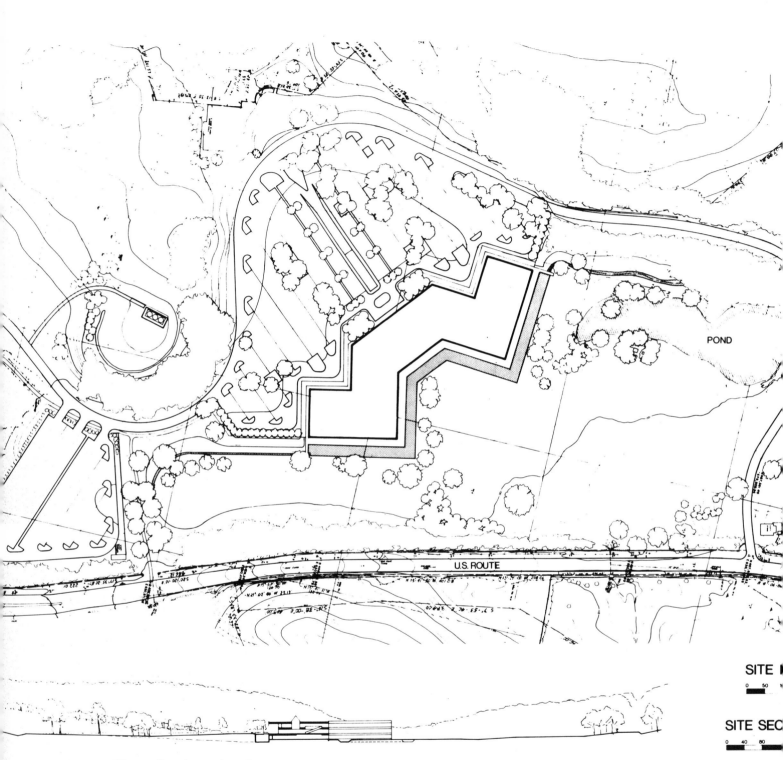

POND

U.S. ROUTE

SITE

0   50

SITE SEC

0   40   80

(Above) Site plan and section.

(Right, top and bottom) The quiet surfaces of the building are reflected in the surrounding moat. Photographs by H. Bernard Askienazy.

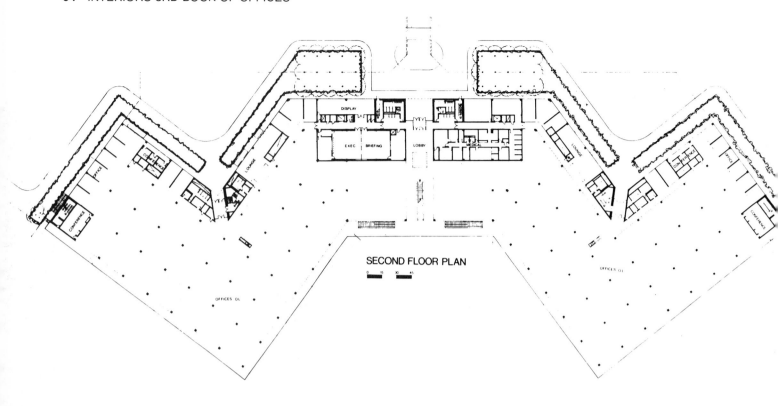

SECOND FLOOR PLAN

Second floor plan. This is the main entrance level and the lower of the two general office floors.

Work station units along the line of perimeter circulation. Photograph by H. Bernard Askienazy.

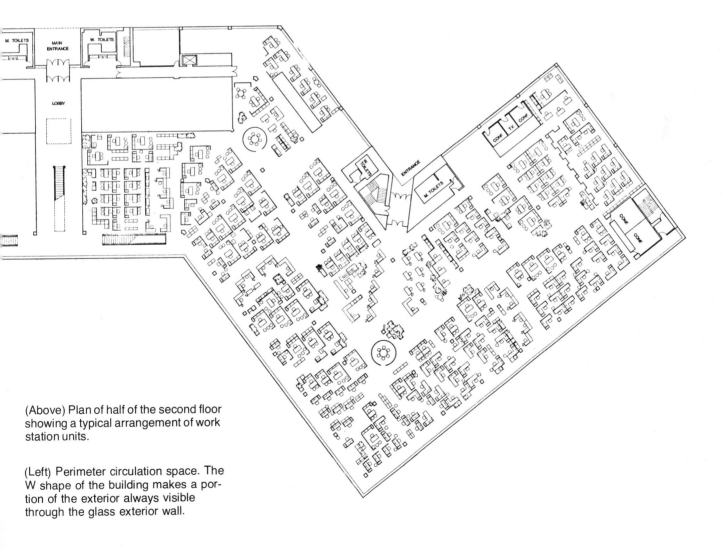

(Above) Plan of half of the second floor showing a typical arrangement of work station units.

(Left) Perimeter circulation space. The W shape of the building makes a portion of the exterior always visible through the glass exterior wall.

Distribution point for the mail conveyor system.

(Right, top) Employees' dining room on the lower level. Photograph by H. Bernard Askienazy.

(Bottom) Conference area with Chermayeff & Geismar wall display taking the role of a painting.

Benton & Bowles

New York, New York
Space Design Group (Marvin B. Affrime, Director), interior designers

The Space Design Group, having become known as something of a specialist in advertising agency offices (this was their eighth such project), made an extraordinary effort to stamp this facility with a unique character. The offices occupy eight floors — about 200,000 square feet/18,600 square meters—at the top of a new Third Avenue building and house some 860 employees. The building architecture establishes a rectangular slab floor, but the stairs, elevators, and services that are usually found in a core are near one end of the floor and on the perimeter wall in this building. The windowless central space is turned to good use in conference rooms, screening rooms, and other special-purpose facilities on the floors where they are needed. On the floors where offices predominate, a central corridor feeds through to give access to inner offices in a way reminiscent of the inside room–outside room pattern typical of an ocean liner's decks.

The Space Design Group studied Benton & Bowles's existing offices and the ideas of its people in great detail in an effort to identify the special character that the agency wanted to express. The key goal was to change the somewhat conservative image that had been identified with Benton & Bowles into a more aggressively creative image. Building standards, with their implications of uniformity and grayness, were avoided and replaced by standards developed especially for this office. Perhaps these are not dramatically different from the norm of quality high-rise office space, but certain small matters make these floors take on a special character. Thin, black-line elements turn up in contrast with white or neutral backgrounds in many places (the edges of doors and openings, intersections of wall and ceiling planes, and the edges of screens set in walls) and establish a certain crisp linearity. Color is used sparingly, but is clear and intense when it occurs. Most unusual of all, fluorescent light is scarcely used, so that its tendency to establish a monotonous bleakness is replaced with the much more varied and warm character of incandescent lighting. There are no ceiling lights in corridors and the combination of wall lighting, color and graphic elements, and careful planning to introduce turns and breaks eliminate the endless, monotonous hall almost completely.

There are three interconnecting stairs within the space. One is a spectacular spiral connecting the two topmost (so-called creative) floors. One is an open rectilinear stair connecting the administrative and executive floors. The third is a continuous stair in an enclosed tower (for fire control reasons) extending the entire height of the space. Each stairway has been developed as an individual focal point with its own character — a device for minimizing the monotony of the standard office building floor.

The typical work space is a private office, one window wide. The perimeter of each floor is, in almost every case, a consistent ribbon of such private offices. A few standard furniture and color schemes give these a reasonable amount of variety. The larger (two-window) offices assigned to people on the next rung up the hierarchical ladder were conceived in recognition of the fact of constant change. As account supervisors are switched to different assignments, their office locations need to change. The typical two-window office has an 8-foot/2.4-meter work table with movable file pedestals underneath and a tackboard above. Moving to a new office is merely a matter of moving the files and changing the tackboard display. Colors are neutral except for throw pillows in bright colors, which can be shifted without difficulty.

Top executive offices reflect the personal (and somewhat conservative) tastes of the occupants. Antiques and oriental rugs are introduced to satisfy the desires of the office users, while the architectural basics remain modern and neutral. A certain consistency of character survives, whatever the decorative character, so that the entire space holds up as a planned totality.

Reception area on the 25th floor. All photographs of Benton & Bowles by Bernard Liebman.

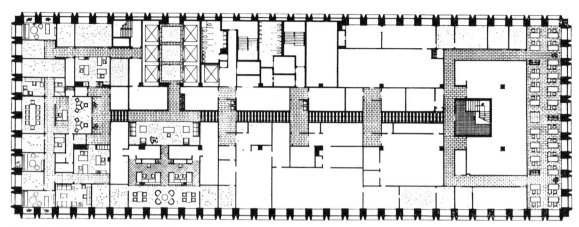

Plan of 25th (office services) floor.

(Above) Reception area on the 28th floor.

(Right, top) Vice president's office on the 29th floor.
(Bottom) President's office.

Reception lobby on the 30th floor.

(Left) Waiting area in executive group on the 29th floor with
stair leading to the account management and merchandising
offices on the floor above.

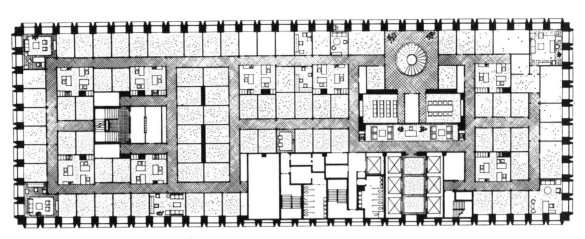

Plan of 32d floor.

(Left) Reception area on the 32d (creative production) floor.   (Above) A viewing room on the 32d floor.

(Left) Reception area on the 33d floor with spiral stair rising from the 32d floor.

(Above) Theater on the 33d floor.

Montgomery Ward and Company Headquarters Building

Chicago, Illinois
Minoru Yamasaki, architect
Sydney Rodgers Associates, interior planners

Montgomery Ward's 27-story, 360,000-square-foot/33,480-square-meter office building is probably the largest entirely open-plan office facility to be tried in the United States. Ward's began experiments with open-plan areas some years ago (with results that were not encouraging at first) and asked Rodgers to start preliminary studies about 6 years before this project was completed. There was close collaboration between Rodgers and Yamasaki in the design of the building, which is, as a result, highly suitable for open offices. The building mass is a simple rectangle with long walls of glass and a minimal number of interior columns in two widely spaced rows. The massive pylons at each end house elevators (all passenger elevators at one end), stairs, toilets, and other services so that the open office areas can be totally without interruption. The pylons are windowless, except for a single vertical strip window on the center-line, and are sheathed in travertine.

With the exception of the fourteenth (diningroom) and twenty-sixth (executive) floors, all the floors are basically alike. In the lower half of the building a conference room near the elevator lobby is the only interruption of the open space—and even this element is eliminated in the upper floors, where it is moved into the pylon area where the lower elevator bank has dropped out. The floor layouts are, in general, highly characteristic of landscape planning. Furniture is distributed according to departmental needs with movable curved screens providing some degree of privacy and separation as needed. In most cases, layout is not quite as totally random as is customary in the German prototypes. Although plans are certainly not rigidly geometric, certain patterns of consistency can be sensed and seen quite easily when examining floor plans. Circulation is generally quite clearly defined with a main artery moving lengthwise through the center of each floor and bending slightly to cut off a straight-line vista. Secondary circulation diverges into departmental areas. In the pylon opposite the elevators, there is an employee lounge and rest area with vending machines on every floor.

Furniture is standardized throughout. The Steelcase 9000 group, which had been under development for some time, seemed ideally suited to this project and its use gives the whole space (with the exception of the dining and executive floors) a unified character. Colors are grouped in five schemes based on tonalities of red, rust, blue, gold, and green. These schemes are used in rotation in groups of five floors throughout the building. Desk chairs are of standard color throughout. The aim is to avoid the monotony of a single scheme throughout such a large project, while avoiding the extreme complexity that would arise if a different scheme had been attempted for every floor.

The executive floor departs totally from the standards used elsewhere, but is also open in the sense that offices are not defined by fixed partitions. Each executive is assigned a large area with ample privacy established by furniture elements and by the positioning of secretarial work stations. The two top executives are placed in diagonally opposite corners of the floor. In addition to a large open office and conference area, each has access to space within the end pylons where fully private conference–diningrooms are provided, along with special toilet and storage facilities. Because of the small population of this floor, the central area is very open, with ample space for a large waiting area, as well as the only major enclosed element on the floor—the corporate board room with an elaborate projection facility.

There is a central word-processing station on the thirteenth floor with a system for telephone dictation to this facility from all parts of the building. This helps to keep down typewriter noise through the other work areas. There is also a background sound system to maintain an ideal level and frequency mix of ambient noise to minimize problems of acoustical privacy and possible noise disturbance.

The general success of this project, a huge headquarters building for a major corporation—all planned as open without partitioning of the sort that is the norm in most office installations—must surely indicate that open planning has come of age. No one can suggest that it is the only way to approach a major office project, but it has certainly become clear that it is *one* way that can be as successful as any other. This must rank as the ultimate demonstration project, the project that makes it clear that landscape planning is no longer to be viewed as a fad, a sport, or an offbeat approach to be considered only as an oddity. Until an even more persuasive example comes along, the Montgomery Ward project will stand as the major testimony to the idea that the landscape office is a serious reality.

Board of Directors' room. Photograph by Hedrick Blessing.

Typical furniture (Steelcase 9000 Series) in a demonstration set-up prepared before move-in.

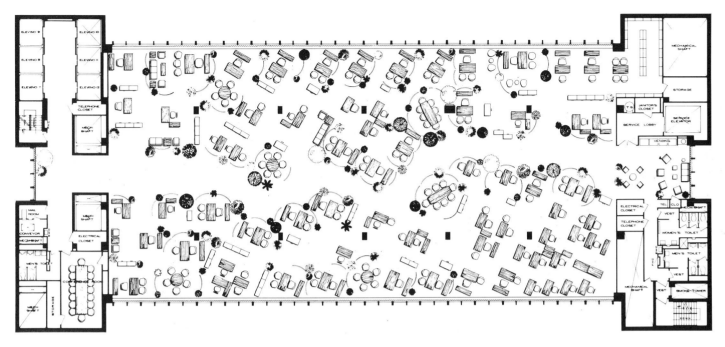

Plan of typical floor.

Occupied working space, typical of the pattern on all the general office floors.

(Above) Typical general office work space. Photograph by
Hedrich Blessing.

(Left) Lines of circulation screened by curved screens and
plants. Photograph by Hedrich Blessing.

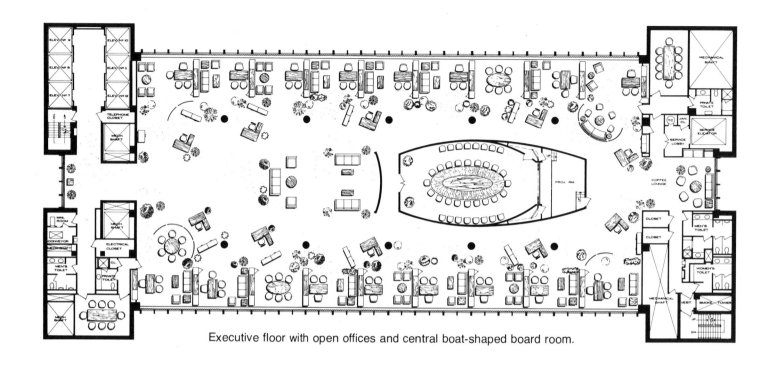

Executive floor with open offices and central boat-shaped board room.

Typical lounge area with vending machines at end of each
general office floor. Photograph by Hedrich Blessing.

(Left) Top executive office in a corner, with private conference space available beyond the solid wall on right. Photograph by Hedrich Blessing.

ARCO Chemical

(A division of Atlantic Richfield Co.)
Houston, Texas
Morganelli-Heumann & Associates (New York Office),
space planners and interior designers
Herbert Bayer, art consultant to ARCO

These offices occupy about three-quarters of a high floor in a rectangular office building. There is a central core for services and all columns are either within the core or at the perimeter glass wall. The major part of the space is a series of private and semiprivate work spaces, with the related secretarial and clerical work stations and files. There is also a general conference room. At one end of the space, where the entire width of the building is available, the interior character changes to accommodate two private offices for high-ranking corporate executives. This area is set off both spatially and by a change in character. The core is extended to the window wall in a visual sense by the location of a glass-walled meeting room. Access to the two executive offices and their related secretarial and waiting space is through a gallery that passes between the meeting room and the end of the core. This planning brings about a carefully developed balance between isolation of this group and unification of the entire space.

In the balance of the space, the three blocks of private offices are distributed along the long wall in a way that does not interrupt the sense of visual continuity of the major work and circulation areas. The space seems to be an example of open planning, although it is actually quite conventional in its provisions for privacy.

Two rather unusual devices increase the sense of visual openness. The ceiling is set at 9 feet/2.7 meters to house mechanical work above, but since the windows rise to a full 12 feet/3.6 meters, a perimeter band has an upward angled ceiling that rises to the top of the glass. This means that as one approaches the window wall, an unexpected increase in view gives a sense of increased space and openness. This sense is further developed by changing solid partitions to glass where they approach the outer wall.

The second unusual characteristic of the space is the absence of the usual grid of ceiling light fixtures. There are no ceiling lights, except for a few incandescent down lights for special purposes and strip lights at the core wall. This is, of course, an indication of an unusual approach to lighting. Task lighting is provided at work stations and general light comes from upward-directed lighting located in furniture. Lighting also comes from chromium tubular light kiosks distributed throughout the space, usually in combination with groupings of plants.

It is interesting to note that rediscovery of this approach to lighting seems to have occurred in response to concern about the energy wastefulness of conventional lighting. The solutions here—lights placed close to work surfaces and low-level, indirect lighting for general circulation spaces — are each approaches with a long history. Task-related lighting must date back to the earliest lighting devices, candles and lamps. Indirect lighting was a discovery of the 1930s that was destined to be pushed aside by the demand for extremely high foot-candle levels throughout every office space. Reversion to the more rational approach used here is both efficient and visually pleasant.

Paintings and lithographs are used in a number of locations to establish visual focal points and introduce color and lively form. They come from ARCO's extensive corporate art collection and are hung here by magnets or on so-called invisible cords from the ceiling so that they can be moved or replaced easily without damage to the walls. The gallery leading to the top executive area also has one wall devoted to a fixed, three-dimensional architectural graphic element that establishes the unique character of that space.

Entrance from the elevator lobby.
Photograph by Jeff Johnson.

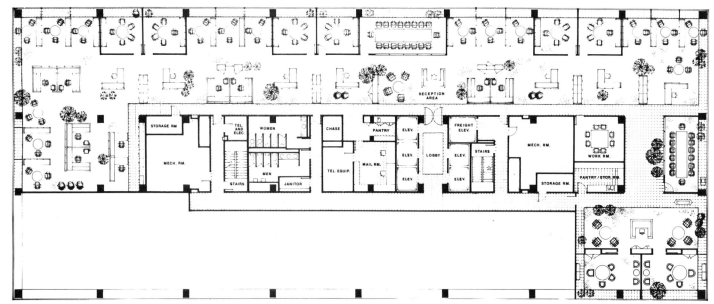

Typical floor plan.

An open conference group. Photograph by Jeff Johnson.

(Right, top) The reception area: receptionist's desk to the left, glass wall of the conference room on right, the open work area ahead. Photograph by Richard W. Payne.

(Bottom) Conference room. Photograph by Richard W. Payne.

A secretarial work station with conference and semiprivate office areas beyond. Photograph by Jeff Johnson.

A typical private office; round table for meetings and work unit against wall replace a conventional desk. Photograph by Jeff Johnson.

In the executive gallery corridor looking toward the two private executive offices. Photograph by Jeff Johnson.

Executive secretarial and waiting area. Photograph by Jeff Johnson.

The corner executive office. Photograph by Jeff Johnson.

(Right) Pantry adjacent to the executive area. Photograph by Jeff Johnson.

Dial Financial Corporation Headquarters

Des Moines, Iowa
John Pile, planner and interior designer

This firm is primarily a consumer load company with hundreds of offices accessible to walk-in customers. Several years ago, as part of an overall corporate identity program developed by Sandgren & Murtha, the firm experimented with customer service offices in which open planning was substituted for the interview cubicles or countered bank-like spaces that had been the previous norm in the field. The success of the experiments led to a changeover (still in progress) of all branch offices to the new approach.

Company headquarters were in a three-story, block-square older building (originally built as a parking garage) and had, over the years, developed into a warren of crowded and partitioned spaces.

The need to add two new offices to the existing executive row led to a study of the building layout in more general terms. A move to a different location was considered, but the economics of the situation (bolstered by an extensive computer installation established on the first floor) led to a decision to stay in the old building, but upgrade the interior to a high standard.

The desire to reduce the sense of crowding in the present space, to provide some expansion space, as well as the favorable experience with the open branch offices led to the adoption of open planning throughout, including the president's and chairman's offices.

The first floor of the building is largely for the computer room, mail room, training rooms, and other services, plus two departments that operate in comparative isolation. The second floor is devoted to space for the systems analysts and programmers who service the computer and, along with it, are the heart of the company's daily operations. The third and top floor houses executives, board room, and the other departmental offices (accounting, marketing, etc.) that have no direct relation to the computer function.

These space location assignments were developed through a survey of personnel and space needs, a rather simplified interaction analysis carried out on the basis of a form submitted to each executive and department head. Matrix diagrams and charts led to a scheme of space assignments that because it was so different from what existed before, came as a shock at first. It was accepted, however, and has proved to be entirely serviceable in practice.

Office work areas are entirely open, uniformly carpeted, equipped with louver-blinds, and lighted with low-brightness fluorescents.

Elevators and stairs are at the outer wall, but a central core is formed by air-conditioning equipment rooms on each floor. The spaces requiring full partitioning, conference rooms, training rooms, etc., are grouped around the core. The balance of the space is an open square. On the second floor, Steelcase 9000 system furniture makes up clusters of workplaces that define work groups. These are in constant flux. Whenever organizational changes take place the equipment is free for rearrangement on an overnight basis.

The third floor is also open and flexible, but with less expectation of constant change. There is a fixed board room floating in the open office space adjacent to the executive area and an enclosed conference room, but all other spaces are open. Wardrobes and files define the circulation ring and define departmental areas to some degree. The executive spaces use Knoll Stephens system equipment, and each executive was involved in layout and color planning for his or her space. In the balance of the floor, Steelcase 9000 furniture is used again, but with more conventional layouts of desks in most departmental areas.

The project includes three quiet rooms — small spaces available to anyone for private conversation or concentrated work requiring total privacy. There is also a phone booth area on each floor for calls that can best be made away from the usual workplace. These provisions, together with generous conference areas, seem to have offset any reservations there may have been about loss of privacy in open-plan space. Experimentally, background sound was omitted at first. It has proved useful only in spaces that were in practice too *quiet* (making overheard conversation distracting). A locally installed sound generator with a concealed ceiling location has been added in these few places with entirely satisfactory results.

The company has moved into a major corporate art program with the guidance of the director of the Des Moines Art Center. Major works in key spots make the space lively and, in some cases, spectacular, and are a source of amazement to company employees.

General work area for programmers and systems analysts on second floor. All photographs of Dial by Norman McGrath.

(Above) Multipurpose classroom, conference room, and meeting room.

Second floor conference room.

Open clerical area on third floor.

Works from Dial's art collection displayed in third floor waiting area.

Executive reception and
secretarial area.

A "quiet" room.

Corner executive office.

Employees' lounge and cafeteria.

Mercedes-Benz of North America (MBNA) National Office

Montvale, New Jersey
The Grad Partnership, architects, with Frank Stiene, staff architect for MBNA
Quickborner Team, management consultants for planning
Hans Krieks Associates, interior designers

Of all the office landscape projects that have appeared in America, this one has the best credentials for being considered an authentic example. The building did not exist before the project, it was not a limited test or experiment, and the concept's originators, the Quickborner Team, were full participants in the design from its beginnings.

All the originators' principles have been carefully observed in this building. From the beginning, programming involved teamwork, with the client's planning team fully involved. Representatives of the client's staff at every level were involved in review and revision of plan proposals as they developed. The design of the building was only undertaken after preliminary concept planning was well along, and the building design is tailored to office landscape requirements. In fact, the total project is a kind of textbook example of what *Bürolandschaft* is in its purest form.

The building houses about 111,000 square feet/10,323 square meters of office space to accommodate 410 people. (Including services, the building has a gross area of 141,000 square feet/13,113 square meters.) The shape is a trapezoid, easily expanded in triangular-hexagonal modules. Column spacing is about 30 feet/9 meters and the work spaces are a clear sweep of open space with central access; services are at the far corners. The ground floor is devoted to services, files, computer and related equipment, a cafeteria, and the public entrance lobby. The main (first) floor above can be entered by staff at ground level and is entirely open-landscape space, except for a walled conference room. The floor above is almost identical, except for a row of five executive offices and their related conference and service spaces. Enclosure of this group seems to be the sole exception to observance of the basic doctrines of Quickborner planning.

In the landscape areas, floors are equipped with a duct system serving access pockets with hinged door covers spaced only 5 feet/1.5 meters apart. Plug-in flexibility for phones and AC is thus virtually total. Simple overall fluorescent light from bare tubes is masked by a baffle system in a triangular grid relating to the building form. The baffles are of acoustical material and are an important factor in controlling noise and cross-talk problems.

A central service station at the access point to each floor provides self-service mail pickup from open trays. Office supply stock is located and distributed here. This service station also houses a copy machine and acts as the floor reception desk. A general file reorganization reduced files to a minimum and then located most file material in central files with an efficient conveyor system to make file retrieval quick and easy. The minimal filing done on the work floors is in open bins. Desks, in the usual sense of the word, are eliminated. The standard work surface is a trapezoidal table that can be grouped to form a variety of larger configurations for meetings as well as for work. Each person is also assigned a special lockable console unit to house private materials, work supplies, and telephone. Some 400 movable screens and 300 live plants round out the usual open office equipment. Carpet color is a warm neutral, furniture surfaces are white with black edgings, but movable screens and the few wall surfaces are in strong, bright colors, giving an overall sense of liveliness. In contrast, the executive offices are subdued almost to the point of being somber, although a glass partition wall looking out into the general office pulls brightness into these spaces as well. The ground floor cafeteria, with a long, uncurtained glass wall, is without bright color, except for a brilliantly colorful mural by Hans Krieks.

In any discussion of the application of open planning in the U.S., this project serves as an ideal yardstick for comparison with the many modifications and imitations of Quickborner practice. This is the authentic standard for the state of the art as the originators now practice it in America. Its acceptability and serviceability for a major industrial corporation with a highly respected reputation is clearly demonstrated here.

Public entrance lobby and display area on ground floor. Photograph by Gil Amiaga.

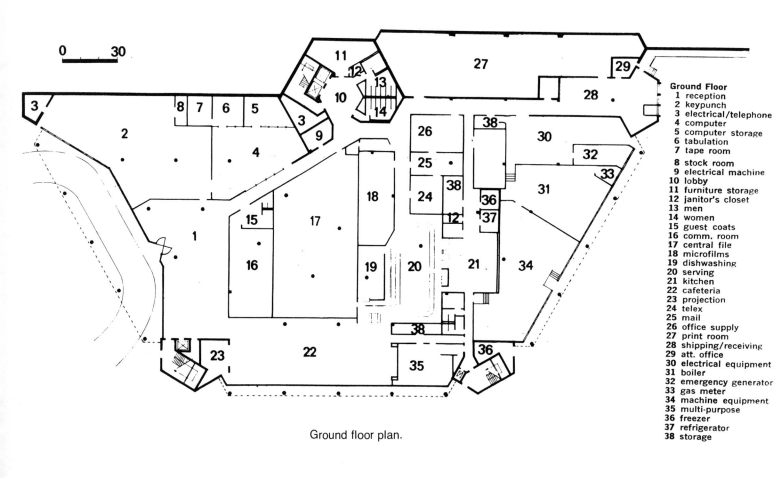

0   30

Ground Floor
1 reception
2 keypunch
3 electrical/telephone
4 computer
5 computer storage
6 tabulation
7 tape room
8 stock room
9 electrical machine
10 lobby
11 furniture storage
12 janitor's closet
13 men
14 women
15 guest coats
16 comm. room
17 central file
18 microfilms
19 dishwashing
20 serving
21 kitchen
22 cafeteria
23 projection
24 telex
25 mail
26 office supply
27 print room
28 shipping/receiving
29 att. office
30 electrical equipment
31 boiler
32 emergency generator
33 gas meter
34 machine equipment
35 multi-purpose
36 freezer
37 refrigerator
38 storage

Ground floor plan.

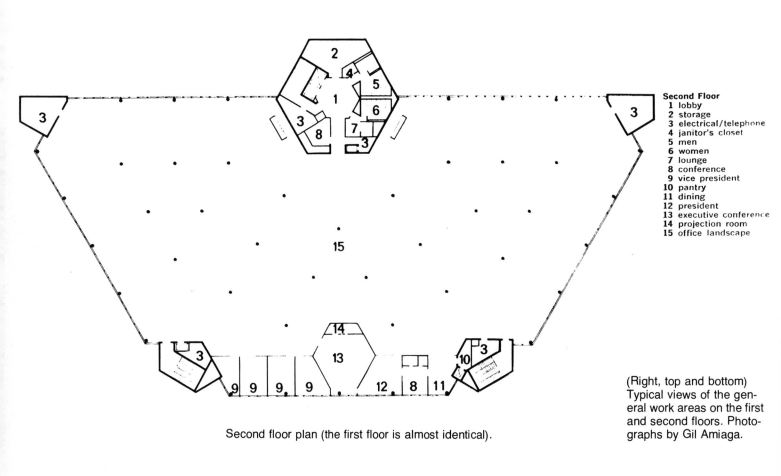

Second Floor
1 lobby
2 storage
3 electrical/telephone
4 janitor's closet
5 men
6 women
7 lounge
8 conference
9 vice president
10 pantry
11 dining
12 president
13 executive conference
14 projection room
15 office landscape

Second floor plan (the first floor is almost identical).

(Right, top and bottom) Typical views of the general work areas on the first and second floors. Photographs by Gil Amiaga.

(Above) General work area
Photograph by Gil Amiaga.

(Right) Close-up of a floor
service station.

(Opposite page, top) A typical secretarial work station.

(Bottom) Floor service station at point of access.

Employees' cafeteria on ground floor. Photograph by Gil Amiaga.

Ceiling baffle system.

Flush telephone and electrical floor outlet closed and open.

The astonishing Victorian mass of
Philadelphia's City Hall makes an ideal
foil for the simplicity of the new Fidelity
Mutual building. All photographs of
Fidelity Mutual by Lawrence S.
Williams, Inc.

Fidelity Mutual Life Insurance Company and Girard Bank

Philadelphia, Pennsylvania
Vincent G. Kling and Partners, architects
Kling Interior Design, interior designers

The new 38-story Fidelity building stands directly across from Philadelphia's General Grant-style, Victorian city hall—each building setting the other off with astonishing contrast. The interior design department of the architect's office was assigned interior responsibility for the banking space at ground level and for the bank's upper-floor offices (as well as the space occupied by two major tenants in the building). In American practice, architecture of office buildings and office interiors are so often unrelated, at least in city rental buildings, that it is both surprising and interesting to see these aspects of a project generated from a common creative source.

The Girard Bank branch occupies glass-walled space at the ground level. A brilliant red-colored, illuminated supergraphic G dominates the space. The carpet is red and magenta and the officers' desks are red. The ball chairs are sufficiently startling, at least in a bank in Philadelphia, to attract surprise and interest on the part of passing pedestrians.

The Trust Department of the bank on the two floors above retreats to a much more conservative flavor. It is not actually of any imitative traditional design, but the wood paneling, conservative chairs, and decorative lamps give it the flavor of older banking offices in a way that is probably reassuring to Trust Department customers.

The Fidelity Mutual Life Insurance Company, co-owners of the building with the Girard Bank, occupy six upper floors. There are nineteen offices for top executives, each different and each developed in response to the occupant's wishes.

The thirty-sixth floor is occupied by an executive diningroom and employee's cafeteria at about the level of the landmark statue of William Penn on the city hall tower. The view of the tower and cityscape beyond make a dramatic backdrop for these spaces.

Above the high-floor dining and conference areas, the building is topped off by a helicopter landing deck!

The branch bank from outside.

Inside the street-level banking space.

(Right) Typical general office space.

(Below) Exhibit area in the executive reception space (35th floor).

(Opposite page, top) The Trust Department.

(Opposite page, bottom) A corner office of a senior officer. The painting is by Elizabeth Osborne.

(Above) President's office.
The painting is by Murray
Dessner.

(Right) The board room.

(Above) The president's dining room on the 36th floor.

(Left) Employees' cafeteria.

Weyerhaeuser Company Headquarters

Tacoma, Washington
Skidmore, Owings, & Merrill (San Francisco), architects and interior designers
Sydney Rodgers Associates, space planners

This spectacular corporate office building is a long, thin bar set like a bridge, or rather a dam, across a small valley in its beautifully landscaped, 230-acre suburban setting. Parking lots at either end are on high ground — the fourth-floor level where entrances occur at both ends of the long strip of the building's mass. This floor is devoted to reception, lounge, dining, and meeting functions. Below, the major working office areas are banked in three levels, each successively wider and shorter as the building moves down into the valley. The steps of width change form the long terraces on both sides of the building that give it its external character. A fifth floor above the entrance level houses the top executive spaces.

The 358,000-square-foot/33,294-square-meter space within the building houses some 830 employees in partition-free, open space. On its completion, this was the largest project to use the landscape concept in the United States and it remains one of the most spectacular applications of the idea so far. Since open planning is so heavily dependent on furniture and screening elements for its character and since the designers were not fully satisfied with any of the available furniture systems for this use, an effort was initiated in which SOM worked closely with Knoll International to develop a new system specifically for this project. The Knoll Stephens system (which has since become a regularly catalogued Knoll product group) makes use of oak-veneered panels that assemble with a connector system. Worktop and storage elements can be added on and fabric-faced acoustical panels can be attached to vary the wood exteriors. As a lumber producer, Weyerhaeuser had an obvious interest in the prominent use of that material. Thus while the building structure is concrete, the external ribbons of concrete become a quiet setting for the constantly visible wood surfaces of exterior walls and equipment. The long gallery corridors that stretch the 570-foot/171-meter length of the multipurpose fourth floor are floored in maple with brightly colored carpets at intervals to relieve the long, uniform vista.

The three working office floors are essentially open lofts — carpeted, lighted, and acoustically ceilinged. Working arrangements are made up entirely from arrangements of the Stephens system elements placed in generally rectangular order with circular conference areas where needed. There is no fixed planning; layouts have been changed several times and changes continue to take place as needed, exploiting one of the prime advantages of open planning—its total flexibility.

The fifth floor houses fifteen top executives and their related staff. Enclosed fixed blocks house a conference room and a briefing room, an alternative to the usual formal conference or board room. Movable chairs and small tables give this space more the character of a lounge or livingroom than the formality of the usual huge-tabled board room. The ends of the building beyond these blocks are a lounge and diningroom, respectively. The remaining central space is as open as the lower office floors, with the territory of each executive defined by placement of units of the same Knoll furniture system. Across each end of the space there is a full-height Helen Hernmarck tapestry of ancient forest images. With the glass walls on either side, the entire space takes on a totally open, outdoor quality.

Each executive's area measures only 9 by 15 feet/2.7 by 4.5 meters, yet the total sense of openness makes these spaces seem extremely generous. The office of the president was originally planned as a space at the end of the floor behind a full partition. In the end he chose to move to an open area comparable with that of the other executives on the open floor.

This project marks a kind of milestone — a rapprochement between the formalities of the corporate headquarters as it has been conceived in terms of architectural monumentality and the new and disturbing doctrines of landscape planning. In the United States, these approaches have seemed to be in irreconcilable opposition. This project demonstrates the reconciliation. Open planning, with all its flexibility and denial of hierarchical status symbolism, here meets the corporate symbol as monumental building in a park, and in some way, both values survive.

A forest scene tapestry by Helen Hernmarck, one of two at the ends of the central space on the executive floor. All photographs of Weyerhaeuser by Ezra Stoller © ESTO.

(Above) Access galleries stretch the length of the building on each side of the fourth floor. Carpet in bright colors breaks the long vista of maple flooring.

(Left, top) A native rock makes a sculptural accent outside the main entrance point.

(Bottom) The helicopter landing pad near the entrance point on the next-to-top floor.

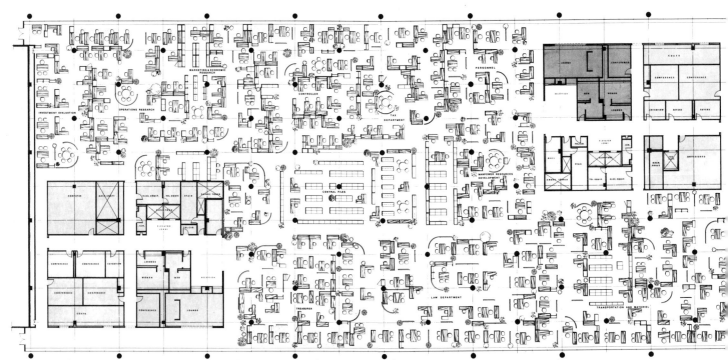

A portion of a typical floor plan of the general office areas shows open planning on a geometric, rectilinear grid.

The central circulation, secretarial, and waiting area on the executive floor.

(Right) General office space.

A typical executive work space.

(Above) Open executive lounge area with fireplace.

(Left) The "executive briefing room" with movable furniture in place of the usual board room central table.

The cafeteria.

Employees' lounge outside the cafeteria with Mark Adams tapestry.

SPECIAL-PURPOSE OFFICE SPACES

The term "office" has a number of meanings. In addition to the complete organizational headquarters that has become the prototypical office project, there are other kinds of offices. Terms such as "box office," "ticket office," or even "post office" suggest a window or counter where the public can come to conduct a special kind of business. Of this public service counter type of facility, the most ubiquitous in recent years has become the bank, not named an office at all, but actually another form of public office. Banks are involved in a continuing process of evolution away from the older image of a fortresslike architectural block built to shelter the inner sanctuaries of cages and vaults. Banks are now moving toward a state in which the architectural reality of the bank will melt away and only the service function will remain. At present this evolution is only half accomplished; the bank is still an architectural identity most often expressed through many branches, local offices that service what the banking industry calls "retail banking." Such banks are important as both service and symbolic representation for the rather abstract reality of a particular bank's image.

The ticket office shares some of the same characteristics, but the services and organizations it represents are somewhat more tangible, and possibly more suitable to direct competitive selling in the manner of a retail store.

The brokerage office is another special case. It shares the role of public contact point for a rather abstract service, but it is also a work space for a complex and specialized activity that demands space and equipment of a unique kind.

The offices of designers and architects are also treated here as special types, partly because the inclusion of a drafting room as a major element makes them unique and partly because, as situations in which the designer is his own client, they become special showcases for ideas about design and planning.

We also include in this section a number of special spaces extracted from context in complete projects because they have aspects of special interest in function, planning, or visual design. While office planning and design can sometimes seem monotonous and unimaginative, examples of situations in which the project or the designer's imagination have gone beyond stereotypes are constantly appearing. They are evidence that there is always the possibility of a new approach that can modify routine and possibly show the way to new and different directions for designers.

Main banking room of Philadelphia National Bank seen from the lounge area at one end. Space Design Group, interior designers. Photograph by Bernard Liebman.

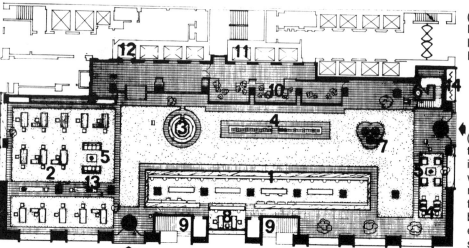

(Above) The mezzanine of the Philadelphia National Bank overlooking the main banking room. Photograph by Bernard Liebman.

(Left) Plan of the banking floor: (1) teller island, (2) officers platform, (3) information, (4) check writing, (5) waiting, (6) stairway to first floor mezzanine, (7) planters, (8) head teller, (9) stairway to subway, (10) building lobby, (11) building elevator, (12) bank elevator, (13) sculpture, (14) window display.

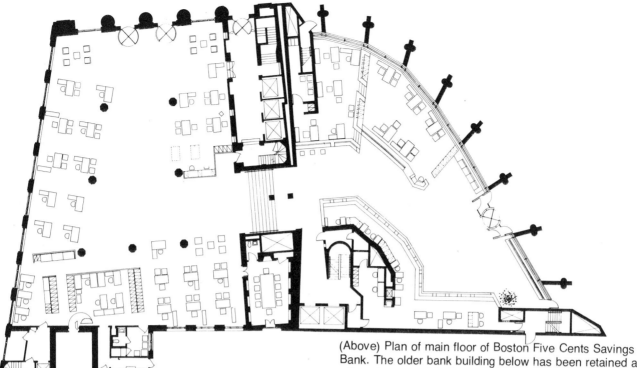

(Above) Plan of main floor of Boston Five Cents Savings Bank. The older bank building below has been retained as officers' space while the main banking area occupies the irregular space in the new building designed by Kallmann & McKinnell, architects, to make use of the site generated by redevelopment of the area. ISD, Inc., interior designers.

(Below) The new main banking hall of the Boston Five Cent Savings Bank. Photograph by Ezra Stoller © ESTO.

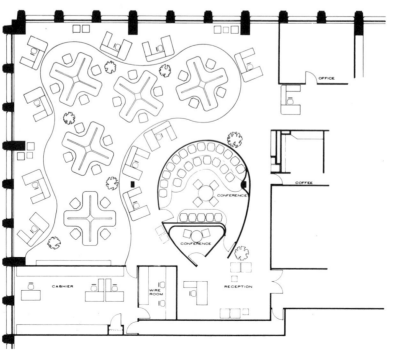

(Above) The general sales area of Lehman Brothers' Houston, Texas, offices with a work station cluster in the foreground. The broker's chair is a standard seat from a Citröen automobile adapted to office use. S. I. Morris Associates, interior designers and space planners.

(Left) Floor plan shows freely placed clusters of brokers' work stations grouped around the oval conference unit.

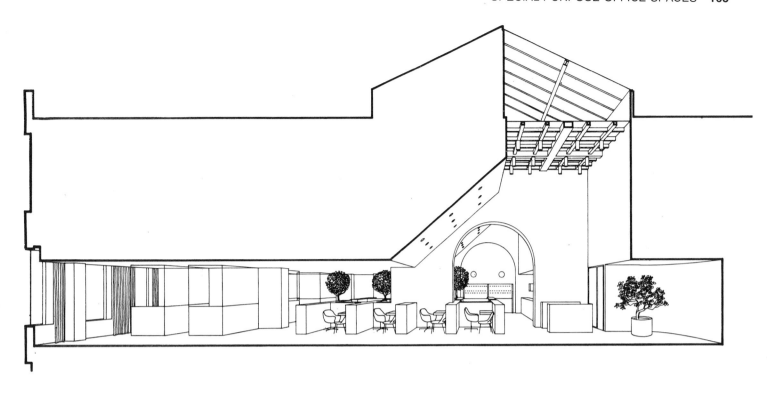

(Top) Section of Shearson, Hammill offices in Seattle, Washington, shows the arch and skylight. These features were made possible by some unusual constructional elements that survived from the former use of the space as a theater. Cambridge Seven Associates, architects and designers with Brown/McCurdy/Nerrie, interior designers.

(Above) Plan shows entrance at (1) and public board room at (2).

(Right) General view of the main work area. Photograph by Julius Shulman.

The spectacular three-story high main trading room of the
Chicago Produce Exchange. I.S.D., Inc., interior designers.
Photograph by Jaime Ardiles-Arce.

(Right, top) Reception area of the I.S.D., Inc., Houston
offices. The firm was, of course, its own interior designer.
Photographs by Robert Muir Associates.

(Bottom) Counter and work stations in the drafting room.

L.C.P. Associates' own offices in New York. The space on the ground floor in the Tudor City apartment complex preserves some existing features of the building such as the vaulted ceilings and leaded-glass windows, visible in the background of this conference room. Photographs by Robert L. Beckhard.

(Right) In the L.C.P. Associates' drafting room, in contrast, everything is new and fully contemporary.

(Above) General view of the Caudill Rowlett Scott office
space with integral ceiling lighting and acoustical treatment.
Photograph by Ezra Stoller © ESTO.

(Left) Caudill Rowlett Scott office building, Houston, Texas.
The sloping site permits a one-floor work space on the lower
level with parking space on the roof. The tower houses the
roof access. Designed by the architects for their own use.
Photograph by Jim Parker, CRS.

(Right) Saphier, Lerner, Schindler Environetics' own office in Chicago. Plan shows irregular space on a mezzanine of the building's public lobby.

(Opposite page) Project directors' room is at a diagonal to the building structure. The building column has been mirrored and makes a kaleidoscopic variation in the visual quality of the space. Photographs by Louis Reens.

(Below) The reception area is open to the lobby when the wide roll-up door is open during business hours.

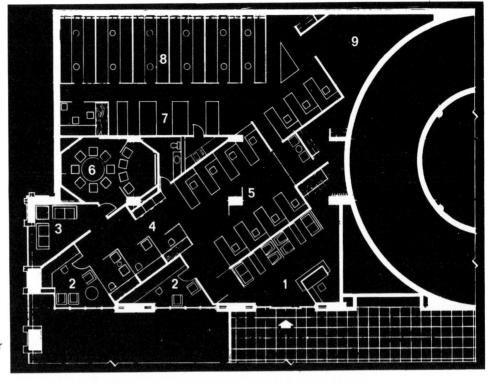

1 reception off lobby
2 private offices
3 conference
4 project analysts
5 project directors
6 presentation
7 designers
8 technical
9 reproduction and file

Lounge–conference seating (foreground) surrounded by
open office facilities in Xerox International Center for Training and Management Development, Leesburg, Virginia.
Vincent Kling & Partners, architects; Kling Interior Design,
interior designers. Photographs by Tom Crane.

(Right) Xerox dining area with clerestory and overlooking
balcony.

SOME TECHNICAL ISSUES

It is neither appropriate nor possible in a book of this size and scope to include a full discussion of the technical matters that office design involves. Planning methods, computer applications in planning, heating and air conditioning, lighting and acoustics are each subjects large enough to have their own literature and their own group of consultant experts. In each of these areas certain standards, customs, and habits have grown up and become routine.

Within the last few years, and since the appearance of *Interiors Second Book of Offices*, there have been several striking developments that influence these areas in such important ways that they deserve special discussion here. Three main influences have brought about unusual change. One is the gradually increasing application of computers. Not only are computers a factor in offices, but they have also become a factor influencing office planning. Planners are experimenting and learning ways in which computers and computer techniques can help, change, and possibly improve office planning. The second influence is the impact of open planning. With open or landscape plans, needs change. Certain old problems are diminished or disappear, but certain new problems surface and call for new solutions. The third factor has been the arrival of the long-predicted energy crisis. Power costs, always thought of as a minor and inevitable factor, have become anything but minor. Ideas that have been waiting on the sidelines for years have suddenly come to the fore when they are able to offer help in reducing energy requirements for the modern office.

Developments are occurring rapidly in each of these areas so that whatever is written today will probably become obsolete within a few months or years. Nevertheless, it seems necessary to include a short report on the changes that are taking place and some discussion of what may be expected in the immediate future.

Method in Office Design

Within the last few years there has been an upsurge of interest in what is often called "methodology" in the world of design. Office planning (along with factory planning) seems to be a design field particularly well suited to the application of organized planning techniques. The influence of the Quickborner Team, strong exponents of a particular method, and of such organizations as The Design Methods Group, an organization of designers from all fields with an interest in methodology, has pushed ahead a new concern for clarity in method.

Architects and designers, like most artists, have been traditionally distrustful of any attempt to define their methods of work. Intuitive creativity has been regarded as a mysterious, indefinable quality that must be nurtured and that may be devalued by any effort to define its processes in an explicit way. The designer, asked how he achieves his results, will usually state that he works in ways that he has learned through long training and experience and that his results must speak for themselves. In the world of business, such answers are not likely to be regarded as totally satisfactory. Businessmen are accustomed to striving for objectives that can be quantified; they often deal with engineers and accountants and are used to their sharply defined values and techniques for pursuing these values. The wide acceptance of functionalism in modern design was a first step away from insistence upon purely artistic values. Little by little, designers have become increasingly willing to accept the idea that design projects can and should have sharply defined aims. The program, a statement of objectives, is generally regarded as a necessary starting point for every planning project; design proposals can be evaluated on the basis of their success in satisfying the program. Nevertheless, the creative steps have tended to remain hidden and undefined even within this context. Because of the vast number of interactive values set forth in almost any program, most designers will still insist that only an intuitive jump from program to design proposal made within the mind of the designer can have any chance of producing a proposal that has any hope of satisfying the program.

Meanwhile, the development of the electronic computer and the techniques of data processing have surfaced. The scientific community was the first to develop and use these techniques, but it has been business that has really put these developments to full use. Every business is now aware that massive and complex data can be dealt with in an astonishingly efficient manner by computers. In learning to put computers to work, business has learned that almost any problem can be processed if the exact steps to be taken are defined in a clear and orderly way. This naturally leads to the realization that design problems must also be susceptible to this approach. It is this line of thinking that has led to a connection between design methodology and computer techniques. Most designers continue to doubt that computers will ever be able to solve design problems in total, but the effort to enlist their aid in even the most menial aspects of design work has forced designers to make an effort to define the steps that are taken in solving design problems.

Most design problems remain intractable to computer-oriented attack because of their excessive complexity and because of the unclear objectives that they involve. Conflicting functional, emotional, and esthetic purposes are too difficult to quantify and

place in logical relationships. In office planning (and in factory planning) objectives are generally easier to define — at least this is true of the objectives that are overtly recognized and publicly stated. An office is a place where an organization wishes to accomplish specific things of a definable kind. These objectives have been discussed in a general way in the introductory section of this book. The conclusion that an office is a center for communication and control is a widely accepted statement. The only purpose of an office is to bring people together in one place where they can communicate with each other and have access to the other instruments of communication and control — paper, telephones, business machines, etc. It is this view that allows us to propose an extremely clear set of values for office planning. Within this view the *only* value that need concern us in office planning is the placement of work stations to optimize ease of communication. People who must communicate a great deal must be close; those who do not need to communicate need not be.

Now at first glance this seems to be a truism that designers have recognized and acted on for years. In fact, it is not so at all. We know that an office plan will often group people by rank (all executives together, all bookkeepers together, for example) or for other values (the president must have a corner office on a high floor), even if these conflict with communication needs. Also, as organizations grow large, communication needs grow hard to remember and process, even if they are known and given priority over other values. No planner can hold in his mind the identities and interrelationships of 2,000 individual people—in fact it is common knowledge that there is a limit of about 150 or 200 people that the mind of one planner can cope with. Larger numbers are ordinarily dealt with by forming groups, within which the individuals are not considered as separate entities.

Modern methods propose to deal with these problems in orderly ways. We can collect the data on the communication needs of any number of people, however large, and store this information. Then, if we can define our planning objective in terms that are quantifiable, we can put a computer to work searching for a layout that will best satisfy the values we have set. What this means in practice can probably be best explained by describing a tiny problem that can still be managed by the mind of one person. The same process can then be understood, when it takes place on a larger scale, with the computer's aid.

Let us suppose that we are to plan an office for a small organization of sixteen people as well as a reception lobby, which we will assume to share the location of the receptionist. We can now make a survey of our staff of sixteen, asking each person to state his or her need for communication with each of the others (the receptionist will also stand for all outside visitors, since they arrive at her desk). If we mistrust the ability of each person to judge these needs, we can substitute more objective measures—the number of actual visits, calls, or written communications made within a given period. In this way we obtain a list of numerical values that express each person's need to be near each other. Thus the relationship between any two people is represented by two figures (A's need to be near B, and B's need to be near A). In a perfectly objective survey, these figures will be the same. If judgment is involved, the two figures may be different and can be resolved by averaging. Display of this data can be set out in a matrix chart. The numbers that fill the chart may be actual numbers of communications or values from a scale such as:

0 No communication
1 Little communication
2 Some communication
3 Frequent communication
4 Constant communication

Using letters to identify people, we can then make a chart that might look like this:

	A	B	C	D	E	F	G	H	I	J	K	L	M	N	O	P
P	0	4	2	2	1	3	1	4	0	0	1	2	3	0	1	
O	1	0	0	1	0	0	0	0	1	4	0	1	3	2		
N	4	3	2	3	2	2	1	0	2	3	3	1	4			
M	3	3	2	3	2	1	1	1	4	1	1	0				
L	0	0	0	1	1	4	1	3	2	1	3					
K	3	2	3	1	1	4	3	2	1	3						
J	2	2	2	4	3	4	1	2	3							
I	3	3	4	3	2	1	0	0								
H	4	3	2	3	1	4	3									
G	4	3	3	3	1	0										
F	0	0	0	1	0											
E	2	3	3	2												
D	1	0	1													
C	2	2														
B	4															
A																

It can be seen easily that even this small chart contains a quantity of information that the human mind cannot hold or manage very readily. A next step in the planning process is to represent the floor space in which this group will be housed in some simplified way. It is convenient to assume that the space as-

signed to each person will be equal. We can then diagram the space as a rough representation of its actual layout. A square space would be

Other shapes might be represented as

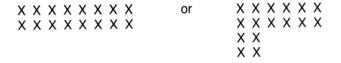

Each X in these diagrams represents a possible location for one person. Each X also has a spatial relationship to each other X. We might call these relationships "adjacent," "near," and "far." We can then give each relationship a numerical value:

Adjacent 3
Near   2
Far   1

Thus, if we place a person in the upper lefthand corner of the square layout, the relationship value for every other person will be:

x 3 2 1
3 3 2 1
2 2 2 1
1 1 1 1

If every other person is assigned a location, we can now calculate the success of the layout with respect to the person at the upper left by multiplying the figure from the matrix that indicates the need for communication by the figure from the plan chart that represents the degree of proximity offered for each other person. This might be called a "figure of merit" for the relationship between the person at the upper left and each of the other fifteen individuals in the organization. Adding these fifteen figures of merit together gives a value for the success of this plan, insofar as the person at the upper left is concerned. We can now do this for each other person in the layout, add together all the quotients, and have a total figure of merit for the entire plan. The reader can probably now guess the next step—to set out every possible plan arrangement, evaluate each by this means, and select for use the plan that scores best. With only sixteen people and sixteen locations available, this seems to be a reasonable possibility. But if the reader is inclined to try it out he must be cautioned that the number of plans possible is no less than 20,922,789,888,000. This staggering number is "factorial 16" (written 16!), that is, 16 x 15 x 14 x 13 . . . etc., on down to 1. Since the number of multiplications and additions that must be done for each trial is not small, it is clear why such techniques lead to the use of computers. In fact, with only sixteen positions under discussion, it hardly seems worthwhile to use such a method. With 1,600 positions it could be helpful, but factorial 1,600 (1600 x 1599 x 1598 . . . etc.) generates a number of trials that will defeat man and machine alike. Nevertheless, it is such approaches that computer-aided methodologies are based on. If we return to our simple example, it is clear that any intelligent planner would shortcut the need to try every possibility. He would instead begin by grouping the individuals who had major need for closeness and would then try schemes that clearly have a possibility for generating high scores. Just a few trials will lead to good results, although the best possible result may be hard to assure. Much the same techniques can be built into computer programs so that, starting from random plans, the computer will be led quickly to evaluate plans that generate good scores. A number of plan diagrams that score well then become available for study by conventional planning methods.

It is possible to "plan in a green field"—that is, with no limitations on spatial configuration—or to demand plans that are fitted to actual space with detailed layout characteristics only slightly abstracted. The diagrammatic plans generated in this way are sometimes quite conventional and would have come to the planner's mind unaided. However, they may also be highly original and surprising, as the methodical program responds to realities that have gone unobserved as a result of habitual ways of thinking. For example, the mailroom may belong at the heart of the scheme, not in the basement; the corner office may be the worst place for the president.

Another approach to methodological planning may seem less comprehensible at first, but has many things in common with the approach described above. In this system, each person, each function, or each department is subjected to a communication analysis similar to that described above. The numbers belonging to each unit in the matrix (those in the horizontal line and the vertical column relating to the item) are added up to given an index of interaction for each unit. The three units with the lowest scores (those least related to all others) are then placed in an equilateral triangle on a coordinate grid plan. Each other unit is then placed on the same coordinate grid in a position determined by vector analysis as the location that will be optimum in relation to the units already placed—that is, in terms of distance from the other points multiplied by need for proximity, as expressed in the rating figures described above. In this approach, real distances are used rather than the simplified rating of proximity. A chart is thus generated, without relationship to any actual space plan, in which each person or unit is placed in an abstract triangular space at a location that is optimum to its communication and proximity needs. This technique uses more subtle mathematical techniques and generates more theoretical results, but has a comparable ability to suggest plans that have a basis in a rationally determined logic, rather than in intuition and guesswork.

The success of such methods is still a matter for considerable debate. The methods generate results that take into account only those considerations on which they are based. Intangible values, preferences, and prejudices, all of which influence human planning, do not enter unless they are articulated and factored into the programs that are to be used. It is often said that a skilled, experienced planner will arrive at the same results or better results quickly and easily, or that the method-generated results are often obviously absurd. As yet, no one suggests that plans generated by such methods can be used uncritically, but many planners, when faced with large and complex projects, welcome the charts and diagrammatic plans that these techniques produce as an aid, a form of suggestion or proposal, which can be used as a basis for development, revision, and a source of stimulation.

If computer-aided planning remains a technique of limited acceptance, several other computer methods seem to have more certain roles, at least in projects large enough to make conventional techniques inadequate. The most obvious of these is the use of a computer as a data storage bank. The mass of information on which a large project is based—names, space requirements, equipment inventories, and needs—can become overwhelming. In addition, since it is subject to constant change, this information can be almost impossible to manage. By using the familiar devices of punched cards or magnetic tape, all such data can be put in a form for compact storage, easy updating, and easy access by CRT (cathode ray tube) or printout. No design organization needs or can afford a large computer, but time-sharing access to a computer by way of a small terminal makes it possible for even a small firm to use a distant computer to store data and make it available in the forms and at the times needed.

A second possibility that has theoretical acceptance in most places (but less general use so far) is the use of the computer as a drafting aid. The key final product of the planning process is drawings—drawings that are large, complex, and based on huge masses of data and decision making. The making of these drawings and their constant revision as the planning process goes on traditionally depended on a rather archaic hand skill—the technique of the draftsman who endlessly repeats the drawings of similar symbols in new configurations. A computer can control the operation of a drafting machine (called a "plotter") so as to make drawings of fantastic complexity at lightning speed. A yet-to-be-made drawing can be stored in computer memory, displayed on a screen, and altered by instructions given through a keyboard and light-pen until every aspect of the future drawing is correct. The actual drawing can then be automatically produced as a tracing or print. Changes and revisions can be made instantaneously through the input devices and new tracings or prints generated as needed.

Such techniques depend on complex equipment and programming and therefore are not economic for projects of small or medium size, but as projects grow larger, their value increases. Architects and designers look forward to a time when perspectives, even motion-picture views of movement through a space, will be instantly available, automatically generated from plans and other data held in computer memory banks; standard elements and standard details will be inserted into developing drawings without effort; new details and new configurations will be entered into computer memory as they are developed and will be available for instant recall as needed. All of this is currently quite possible, but widespread use is limited by the complexity and cost of the necessary equipment and by the limitations of the programming developed to date—which is itself often more complex and more costly than the equipment it serves.

Method is not, of course, necessarily synonymous with the use of computers. In fact, it may well be that the most important value of the computer-oriented methods is the way in which they have forced clarity in thinking about the more conventional method of design. If communication and issues of adjacency are not the only values that need to be considered in office design, the designer is pressured to identify and define the other issues, explain their roles, and assign them weights. Bringing these matters out of the haze of intuition and artistic talent and into a clear light,

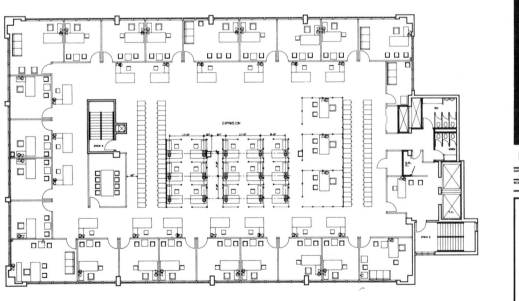

An example of computer drafting: a plan produced automatically by the SLS Environetics computer-driven plotter.

where designer and client can study them, is surely a healthy and constructive development. Unusual schemes that may prove to be highly advantageous are far more likely to be generated under such circumstances, and the understanding that must usually precede their acceptance demands that they be based on a clear and comprehensible rationale. Method is nothing more than the thoughtful pursuit of good information and rational ways of permitting this information to lead to good solutions to real problems.

Energy Issues

In a line of development that has its origins some 50 to 100 years in the past, the modern office has been becoming increasingly dependent on artificial environmental controls that are energy consumers. Offices, like all building interiors, had relied from the beginning on simple natural means for light, ventilation, and whatever control of temperature a building could offer — until the modern technological revolution began to offer independence from the limitations of these simple controls. Natural light demands a building with windows of adequate size and with a plan that places all work space close enough to these windows to make adequate illumination possible. Natural ventilation is dependent on the same windows, on planning that favors suitable air flow, and on simple devices to control air flow, like vents and stacks. Natural heating and cooling are not totally available in all climates, but intelligent orientation to trap sun, avoid winds, and use suitable materials to provide natural insulation go a long way toward making many older buildings habitable without modern systems of heating and cooling.

Artificial light and heat first appear as marginal aids to natural environmental control techniques. A lamp or light fixture can help late in the day or on a dark winter day. A stove or furnace can help out when sun heat is not adequate. As artificial lighting, heating, and finally cooling devices became better, and as the energy systems that power them became more available and economical, it became increasingly possible to consider a building independently from its natural environment. In fact, the idea of a controlled environment tended to become an ideal with an appeal of its own. Planning could be freed of irritating constraints if windows could be made incidental or eliminated altogether. Comfort could become something absolutely controlled by mechanical systems without reference to climate, location, or orientation.

As the sealed building — which was windowless or had windows only as incidental esthetic concessions — became more common, misgivings about the success of this approach began to arise in various quarters. Most often these misgivings were expressed by building users in minor roles — the occupants of internal cells artificially lit and conditioned but strangely unpleasant and confining, in spite of their supposed ideal environmental controls. These misgivings did not gain much attention, however, until in a surprisingly sudden way the much-discussed energy crisis emerged. This came as a result of an oil fuel crisis at a time when demand was outstripping the supply of energy — energy that was generated through the consumption of irreplaceable fuels in most cases. It was the economic impact of this energy crisis that focused attention on the realization that the buildup in energy dependence for environmental control was, in fact, totally unnecessary and simply the result of a habit, furthered, perhaps, by the energy suppliers' enthusiasm for increasing energy demand as long as supplies seemed to be unlimited.

Almost within weeks, standard practice in planning office environmental control became obsolete. Yet, a return to natural light and ventilation and a minimization of energy-dependent heating and cooling systems still seem to be difficult for the modern architect, designer, or client to consider. Most developments in energy management, insofar as they concern office buildings, are still at the level of trying to improve efficiency in energy use in systems that are still largely based on an assumption that office space must be artificially lighted and heated.

There is no sound evidence that such artificially controlled interior environments are in any way superior from the point of view of user health, comfort, or work efficiency; there *is* considerable evidence, however, that they *may* be harmful in various ways. It is hard to imagine how costly artificial conditioning can possibly be justified on an economic basis. Yet, our supposedly rational business world has still not seriously considered a return to primary reliance on natural light and air. Surely there is something irrational about a city environment in which office windows must be sealed to keep out dirt and artificial lighting must be provided because natural light is cut off by smog, when the dirt and smog are, in considerable part, generated in the process of providing the very artificial light and air conditioning that the sealed and lighted buildings require. It is a closed system of wastefulness and futility.

In any case, however limited the steps may now be, the efforts at energy conservation that have surfaced recently are steps in the right direction. Details on developments in artificial lighting are dealt with in the following section. The other primary area of research has been an effort to study the problem of heating and cooling in a way that will minimize energy waste. From the point of view of physics, the temperature inside a building will remain unchanged indefinitely unless something changes it. Once an appropriate temperature has been arrived at, no energy is required to maintain it at that level, unless heat is lost or gained in some way. Heat is lost into a colder outside environment through building surfaces and openings —small leaks or larger door openings. Heat is gained, even when the outside air is cold, when sun energy is received; when the outside environment is warmer than the interior, heat is gained through the same building surfaces and leaks that lose heat. Heat is also gained from energy consumption within the building space for lighting and other uses, as well as from the body heat of the occupants. Cooling devices (fans and air conditioners), since they use energy, generate heat that must be disposed of. It is not unusual to find a situation in which an energy-using device (such as an electronic computer) generates heat that is disposed of through cooling systems, which in turn also generate heat that must be disposed of. At the same time a heating system is using energy in producing heat to make up for heat loss through walls and openings. The same heating system is heating the computer so that it requires more cooling, which in turn generates more heat that must be disposed of at further energy cost. Sun heat in winter is cut off by thermal glass, blinds, and sunshades, while natural air circulation in summer is cut off by the same sealed windows.

Not all these problems can be eliminated in any system that demands precise environmental control along with total freedom in building form, placement, and structure. But waste that results from unrelated systems that draw energy simultaneously to cool and heat in the same space can be reduced. Lighting, since it consumes electrical energy, is automatically a heating device. The heat from lights needs to be conserved and used in winter when heat loss is a problem; it needs to be removed and disposed of in summer when heat gain is the problem. Heat from a computer can be conserved and recirculated in winter and removed at its source in summer. Such innovations are not very significant in terms of design and planning; they merely require engineering attention to all energy systems in a building. Heat from lights or computers needs to be drawn into an unpopulated space (ducts or plenum) before it can cause discomfort and where it can be removed when the problem is heat gain; it can be recirculated when the problem is heat loss. Sun heat needs to be excluded in summer, trapped in winter. Such arrangements require devices that can change the pattern of energy balance and distribution with the season, and even hour by hour with the weather and time of day. It is easier to plan fixed systems and provide an excess of heating and cooling to overcome extremes, but it is more costly in energy, and in most cases, no less expensive in terms of first cost.

Of course, it is cheaper to employ logical, rational planning. This should, theoretically, force the logical solutions to be used as time goes on. However, logical action still requires comprehension of what is logical and a willingness to take the time and make the effort to do what is reasonable. Habit on the part of the manufacturers of building equipment and on the part of suppliers of energy, as well as indifference on the part of the professionals who plan building systems, tend to drag down needed developments in this area. Those who are office clients are rarely able to understand the issues involved and so, often follow advice that is based on habit and the desire to sell equipment, rather than on the real need to minimize energy consumption. Every project deserves one or more rounds of special study on the issues of energy conservation in an effort to achieve the best possible results in this area.

Lighting

After thousands of years of almost total reliance on natural light, within a short time a series of inventions have made it possible to artificially light interiors of buildings in a way that is highly satisfactory. The modern office has developed on a time schedule that is almost exactly parallel to the development of modern lighting. By the 1930s, good artificial light was regarded as necessary equipment in any office space, but most often it was thought of as auxiliary lighting for use on dark days or after sunset. Office space totally without daylight has been largely a post-World War II development. Fluorescent light, with its lesser energy demand (as compared with incandescent light), has made artificial lighting less costly both directly and through the lesser heat output byproduct with its load on air conditioning systems. Developments in modern lighting have been undertaken, in almost all cases, by the manufacturers of lighting equipment and by the power companies. Although much research funded by these interests has been useful, there is always a sense that these are "interested parties," interested, specifically, in the view that more light is always better.

Independent research at universities and in independent laboratories has not usually been as well publicized nor as widely translated into usable equipment and systems. It has generally tended to support the view that the quantity of light, except at the extremes of too little or too much, is far less important than quality. Unfortunately, quantity is easy to measure with a simple meter; quality is hard to describe or evaluate.

These conditions have led to a situation in which most offices are flooded with a costly excess of light that is delivered in a way that handicaps seeing and,

An example of the low-brightness fixture using parabolic louvers to redirect light and make the visible surface of the fixture appear almost dark.

incidentally, is more often than not unsightly — or as one may put it, ugly. The human eye is a highly adaptable device, equipped with an iris that adjusts constantly and automatically to light levels, just as the lens of a modern automatic camera adjusts. People can see fairly well by one candle (if it is close enough and well shaded) and they can see well on a beach or ski slope in full sun (if shielded from direct glare). This is a range from a level of about 1 foot-candle or a bit less, to a level of over 6,000 foot-candles. (The foot-candle, the light of a standard candle at a distance of 1 foot/.3 meters, is the usual unit for measuring levels of illumination.) *Any* interior artificial lighting in modern use provides illumination well within this range. It is true that ease of seeing can be increased somewhat, particularly when a difficult task is involved (such as reading fine print or sewing black thread on black material) by keeping light levels up—above 25 foot-candles as a minimum and, as the tasks become more demanding, up as high as daylight levels. But one must be wary of experiments that merely prove that the human eye will accept as much light as it is given. Few experiments attempt to explore how *little* light will serve a given purpose when properly delivered.

In fact, most lighting is excessive in intensity and unsatisfactory in quality. Excessive levels are not, in themselves, harmful; they are only wasteful. But poor quality leads to strain, discomfort, fatigue, eye damage, and, it seems possible, other physical damage. The aspect of quality that is most often neglected and that seems to be the key to successful lighting is "brightness contrast," that is, the ratio of the brightest point in the field of view to the brightness of the main visual task. Everyone has experienced the problem of a bare bulb hanging over a desk or work table, a bright window behind a person being visited, or a glaring sun over the road when driving. We instinctively put up a hand for shade in these situations and hat brims and eyeshades were invented to deal with such problems. The problem arises because the iris of the eye can make only one adjustment at any given time. It can adjust to dim light or bright light, but not both at once. It will attempt a compromise or will alternate between shutting down, to exclude the bright spot and so exclude light needed to see the subject at hand, and opening up, to aid seeing the task and so admitting excessive glare. Shading the bright spot allows the eye to open up for the task at hand without discomfort.

Most office lighting seems designed to demonstrate how uncomfortable excessive brightness contrast can be. The most common modern installation involves a pattern of fixtures in a ceiling—each shows up as a bright spot in a dark ceiling. A meter will show that the fixture brightness is far greater than the brightness of the tasks at desk-top level. The eye can find no proper setting in such a lighting environment. It is only necessary to shield the eyes with one's hands or use an eye shade to cut off the view of the fixtures to make an instant improvement in seeing in any such situation. Over the years, a number of approaches have been taken to deal with this problem. Light tubes can be shielded with louvers of one type or another that permit light to fall downward toward work surfaces but cut off the viewing angles that cause excessive brightness levels. Alternately, a diffusing plane can be introduced below the light tubes to make the entire ceiling a surface of uniform brightness. The first approach can be quite effective if the baffles that cut off view of the light tubes are black or shaped, so as to deflect direct light rays. The black louver approach has now been largely superseded by parabolic louvers offered under various trade names (such as Para-Wedge or Para-Louver) that achieve low brightness at the fixture while conserving light output. A second approach, usually called a "luminous ceiling," after enjoying a wave of popularity, has largely disappeared. It was disappointing for two basic reasons: (1) because the entire ceiling became an area of excessive brightness, although less excessive than the usual individual fixture; and (2) because the problems of maintenance of the diffusing surface and of fire safety were not as easy to solve in practice as had been anticipated.

The modern low-brightness fixture using parabolic louvers provides a practical source of general illumination without introducing excessive brightness contrast. It might be expected that it would become the most widely accepted standard, but actually its acceptance is hampered by the fact that it delivers a lower level of light at the work surface per watt of current consumed than the simpler fixture lacking adequate brightness control. Thus, one can buy more light for less energy if one will accept bad quality. The economic considerations are complicated by the fact that the first cost of the low-brightness fixture is slightly higher than that of the simple fixture. It is actually preferable to accept a lower level of illumination without excessive brightness contrast to meet a cost standard, than to sacrifice quality of light for what seems to be an economy in terms of quantity of light; but this is a difficult point to make clear to most decision makers when the time comes to determine what light fixture to select.

Very recently a new development has surfaced, in the wake of suddenly rising electrical costs and the new realization that energy conservation is an issue of real importance. The ideas behind the concept, called "task lighting," are not new in any way. Home lighting almost never attempts to flood an entire space with a uniform light flux adequate to permit any task at any

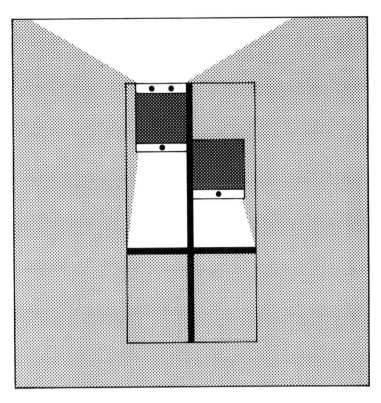

Task lighting in diagram.

An office furniture group incorporating task lighting. Courtesy Knoll International, Inc. Photograph by James M. Fesler.

place in a room. Instead, lamps are placed where needed to light tasks (reading, sewing, etc.), while a spill of light upward is allowed to fill the balance of the space with a lower level of light adequate for movement and other less eye-straining tasks. The logic of this approach arises from a basic physical fact. Light levels vary inversely as the square of the distance from light source to point of delivery. A light in the ceiling that will deliver 50 foot-candles will deliver 200 foot-candles if brought sufficiently close to the surface where it is needed with no increase in cost of fixture or in energy consumed. We are all accustomed to small, local light units as a means of achieving good seeing for specific needs (desk lamp, a piano light, or sewing machine light), yet this idea had been lost with the practice of lighting offices to achieve a uniform, high level of light throughout the space from ceiling sources.

In an office where task lighting has been fully adopted, no ceiling lights are provided (except, possibly, in some special areas such as conference rooms, corridors, or display spaces). Instead, every work place is equipped with local lighting. The fixtures are usually set at a height that ensures comfort for a seated person by cutting off any direct view of the source from below; they also cut off glare to a person standing above. In this way light is delivered downward to work surfaces at a fairly high level and upward to the ceiling at a lower level. If the furniture layout is such that dark areas would result in some places, additional up-light units are placed as needed. Power comes from floor outlets so that the ceiling is not "wired" at all. The ARCO Chemical office, illustrated on pages 116–125, is a good example of this approach. Of course, this approach is particularly suited to open-plan offices, where furniture with integral lighting is distributed fairly evenly throughout the office space. Indeed, one problem of open planning, the possibility that certain desk or screen locations may create shadows, is eliminated when the lighting is directly attached to the work surface.

Adoption of this approach has been slowed down by the need for furniture that includes proper provision for lighting. In first installations, it was necessary to design special equipment and have it specially made, but several manufacturers are now offering standard products designed specifically for this approach and more such systems will, no doubt, appear quite rapidly.

The dominant pressure for consideration of task lighting is economic. Studies indicate that the wattage needed to give satisfactory light levels can be reduced to about 50 percent of that required with conventional ceiling lighting. The reduction in lighting wattage reduces the load on air conditioning so that an additional wattage saving of about 25 percent can be made in that system. Instead of estimating about 5 watts per square foot of office space for lighting, an allowance of 2 watts becomes adequate. There are, of course, related savings in first cost of fixtures and costs for cleaning and relamping.

Aside from economic advantages, the obvious questions have to do with how well this approach works. Do people like it and can they work under the conditions it provides? Unfortunately, full and clear testing of these issues is difficult and has not yet taken place with sufficient controls to be fully definitive. The installations in service are clearly satisfactory to the extent that they are workable in daily use and are delivering the expected savings. Users and visitors who are conditioned to the brilliant flood of light in conventional offices are taken aback at first by the more quiet, almost residential ambience of task lighting. Some people are initially fearful that the light is not adequate, while others feel an immediate liking for the more gentle feeling that this system produces. With the possible exception of workers having special lighting needs (draftsmen and engineers, for example), most users adapt quickly and find the system fully satisfactory.

In any case, major experience with this technique will develop quickly. The General Services Administration (GSA) of the U.S. government has embraced task lighting as a major tool in moving toward its goal of reducing power requirements in all government office spaces to 2.3 watts per square foot. The GSA probably administers more office space than any other single organization in the world and is therefore in a position to produce a vast, highly influential demonstration of how this technique looks and works.

Acoustics

For many years, the issue of sound control in offices has received only the most casual consideration. Traditionally, nothing whatever was done about this matter, except when some painful problem surfaced; then, some minor and often marginally successful corrective action would be taken. Acoustical problems in conventional offices, when they occur, usually fall into two unrelated categories.

1. *Noise control.* A busy office tends to be noisy. Typewriters and other business machines are noise makers, conversation and movement of people and equipment add noise, and as noise levels climb, people must speak more loudly to overcome the background sound. Hard surfaces of tile floors, plaster walls, and hard ceilings reflect sound so that noise can become a major irritation and a hindrance to work. The standard cures for these problems are now well known. Noisy machinery should be isolated in special rooms or, at least, should be padded and

shielded to reduce noise at the source. Ceilings should be chosen for acoustical materials that absorb sound rather than reflect it. Most recently it has become common to carpet floors even in general work areas so that the floor, as well as the ceiling, will become a sound absorber. In almost every case, some combination of these steps will bring office noise down to a bearable level.

2. *Sound transmission*. Conventional office plans include private offices whose purpose is to give the occupant several kinds of privacy—the most important probably being auditory or acoustical privacy. People in private offices want to be assured that their conversations will not be overheard by neighbors, and in turn that they will not hear what happens outside their own space. Unfortunately, the systems used to partition offices and the ceilings commonly in use do not do very well at limiting sound transmission. Walls need weight to be good sound stops, and office partitions, particularly those intended to be movable, are light. They often transmit sound all too easily. Hung ceilings provide open spaces over the tops of partitions through which sound travels easily and air conditioning ducts can act as speaking tubes. These problems are not so easy to solve as those of noise control. Every type of partition is rated as to its sound transmission characteristics; the choice of partitions with good ratings (usually the most expensive types) will help. Sound stops above ceilings and acoustical linings inside ducts can also help. But even when these techniques are used, some disappointments occur. In the end, the best cures for sound transmission problems are planning techniques. The planner needs to consider what spaces are to be adjacent in order to avoid adjacencies that set up problems that will be hard to solve. Isolation of a space by placing it so that it abuts outer walls, fixed building walls, and neutral spaces (like closets, corridors, etc.) is likely to be more effective than any practical amount of soundproofing.

The arrival of the open or landscape office has somewhat changed this limited range of office acoustical problems. In open planning, the entire office becomes like the traditional general office. Noise control becomes vital. Not only an acoustical ceiling, but also a carpeted floor *must* be provided. The ceiling may use baffles or coffers to increase the area of sound-absorptive material; acoustical panels on walls and free-standing screens may be added until sufficient acoustical material is present to drop the sound to a level that will be comfortable. At this point a second problem surfaces. The space may become so quiet that nearby conversations are easily overheard. This may leave the speakers with a sense of inadequate privacy and the nearby workers with an annoying distraction. Without any private offices, there is no place

where additional privacy is available. In practice, these problems are not as serious as they may seem and are susceptible to rather simple control. The first control is once again a matter of planning. Meeting and conference rooms need to be located so that the nearest workers are far enough away to allow sound to fall to an unobjectionable level. Workplaces of managers and executives who have frequent meetings need to be spaced to minimize cross-talk.

The next line of defense lies in the recognition that too little sound can be as troublesome as too much. A very quiet office makes every sound stand out. If the really bothersome sound frequencies (like the click of a typewriter) are diminished, the normal hum of activity can become a background that screens conversations at a short distance. This is like the familiar patter of sound in a pleasant restaurant, where the most private of conversations can readily take place without concern. Proper density of workplaces and proper selection of acoustical and other materials can help to bring the quality and level of office sound close to this ideal. Where this is not achieved, artificial sound may be introduced to solve the problem. It has been obvious for some time that, quite by chance, the mild hiss of air conditioning already provides some of this kind of background masking sound. Where this is not enough, an electronic system can be provided to deliver to ceiling speakers a specially generated sound, a mix of random frequencies designed to mask conversation without introducing irritation. Two approaches have been developed for providing background sound. One uses a central sound generator that feeds local speakers located throughout the space. This is a system similar to (or identical with) that used for background music or public address functions. The same system can serve both purposes, in fact. The sound level can be adjusted by local controls at each speaker, but the kind of sound, the frequency mix in use, will be the same throughout the installation. A second approach uses a self-contained unit that is both frequency generator and local speaker. Such units offer great flexibility in dealing with problems on a local basis. The location and spacing of the sound units can be adjusted while the space is in use, changes can be made easily, and the sound quality can be altered locally as may be necessary to give the best results.

The simplest approach to open-office acoustics is very unsubtle. It is to use a maximum of sound-absorbent materials throughout the space so as to drop noise levels to a point that is *too* low. A background sound system is then introduced throughout the space to put back a uniform masking sound that virtually assures that no acoustical problems will occur. The second approach is more subtle and demanding, but has certain advantages. It is to plan the use of acoustical materials carefully in an effort to arrive at an ideal sound level naturally and then to move into the space with no artificial sound system and to study where problems may occur. Then, at the problem points, background sound can be introduced locally, carefully tailored to the need in terms of level, character, and location. This approach is likely to be less costly and more satisfactory, but demands more effort on the part of the acoustical consultants involved, as well as a willingness on the part of the office users to be patient and cooperative during an initial period of adjustment.

Safety and Security

Until a very few years ago, the twin issues of safety (primarily from fire and possible accidents) and security (from theft and intrusion) hardly required any attention in office design projects. Offices do not deal with dangerous materials, as factories often do, and do not usually contain much of great value to attract thieves. Accordingly, it has been routine to merely comply with local building codes, provide normal locks on doors, and assume that these matters need no further attention.

Unfortunately, various unrelated developments of recent years have changed the picture, and every office project now requires a detailed review of safety and security problems and, in most cases, some special planning to cope with actual or possible problems. Not all the factors that have led to this changed picture affect every office, but some combination of them usually are in the background. Buildings are, in most cases, more open to visitors than ever before. Closed doors and a tiny glazed wicket for the receptionist are not fashionable. In multistory buildings, the replacement of the attended elevator by self-service elevators has removed a key control factor and a group of personnel always present and available to help with all problems of access and exit. At the same time, high and extremely high buildings (above the reach of even high-ladder trucks) have become commonplace in most cities and even in some nonurban locations. The almost universal acceptance of air conditioning has produced sealed buildings with windows that cannot be opened and with a complex system of hidden ductwork and blowers that can distribute smoke and fumes in highly undesirable ways. The trend away from closed private offices has produced vast open areas without natural fire-stop boundaries and with multiple circulation paths hard to place under tight supervisory control. At the same time, the desire for a softer and more comfortable ambience in offices has introduced more imflammable materials — carpet, wood, and upholstery — in place of the earlier substances such as hard flooring, steel desks, and minimal seat padding.

On top of these factors, the new materials turn out to have some unfortunate characteristics in safety terms. Synthetics often burn more easily than the older materials they are replacing, and when they burn or smolder, they often produce toxic smoke or gases that are a hazard even when a fire is minor.

In security matters, a similar combination of circumstances has generated new problems. There has been a sharp increase in crime, particularly in urban areas with major social problems. Offices, now filled with portable, costly, and easily salable business machines, have been identified by thieves as particularly easy hunting grounds. There has also been an increase in the willingness to use direct action as a weapon of social or political persuasion so that almost any organization might, in some future turn of events, find itself under attack.

Certain types of offices—brokerage firms and banks (if we may consider them offices)—are clearly vulnerable and have a history of adopting various protective measures. But even organizations that have no history of problems need to give some thought to these issues when planning new offices.

In matters of safety, legal requirements are being altered and made more rigorous as new fires occur and reveal the problems of modern buildings. It has been customary for owners and tenants as well as their designers and architects to regard such requirements as nuisances or obstructions to be met only grudgingly. This is, in present circumstances, hardly a reasonable attitude. Fire dangers in many modern buildings are very real, and planners need to make a creative effort to minimize hazards rather than to continue to resist and evade existing rules. Designers have a clear responsibility to consider fire safety when choosing furniture and materials. Visibility and accessibility of exits are a planning issue as well as a matter of compliance with rules. Air conditioning systems need a special review for protective features that provide automatic shut-down, fire shutters, and similar arrangements to minimize the hazards they introduce. Provisions of alarms, extinguishers, and enclosures for hazardous materials (tape, film, and solvents are those most often found in offices) are all matters that can best be considered as part of the planning process rather than as afterthoughts.

Subdivision of open space with fire-stop walls is a troublesome problem in open planning, but a useful technique in conventional layouts. Codes (such as New York Local Law 5, with its limitation of a maximum of 7,500 square feet/2,100 square meters for open areas without fire walls) are beginning to place fire control needs above the ideals of the landscape planning theory. The most effective of all fire control methods, a full sprinkler system, has been available for many years and can make all these other issues unimportant. Sprinklers are fully automatic 24 hours a day, and they both detect fire and extinguish it promptly with a minimum of damage. The cost of sprinklers has led to resistance to their use in office buildings, but it is increasingly clear that this is the only real solution, particularly in high buildings. Even the cost may be less of an issue than it appears at first when its effect on other requirements and on insurance rates is taken into consideration.

Compared with fire problems, most other safety issues seem minor, but they are still matters that designers need to consider. Steps, stairways, and their railings always represent safety problems. Glass doors and large glazed wall areas must be marked for visibility. Furniture needs to be checked for sharp corners and edges. File cabinets must not be able to be overturned when several drawers are open at once; this is impossible in good equipment with interlocked latches. The weight that files represent must be considered as a problem for the floor structure.

Problems of security seem to interest occupants of buildings more than issues of safety — possibly because the threats are more personal and so much more frightening. It is in the planning stages that these matters can best be dealt with. Locks and keys are not, unfortunately, a total solution to security problems. Keys must inevitably be made available to many people, and duplicates soon circulate widely. Changing a lock and providing new keys is costly and troublesome. Open lobbies and direct access to office spaces from elevators make difficult problems for lock-and-key protection. In any case, the planner and his client need to review office plans to check every point of access (including service routes, exits, and such unlikely areas as skylights and pipeshafts) to consider how each one is to be controlled both during business hours and in the after-hours times when service personnel are at work and when the building is closed. Minimizing the number of access points is highly desirable so that good control can be established at these areas.

New technology offers various aids with security problems. Locks operated by magnetic cards are more flexible than keyed locks and can solve more problems. Closed circuit TV can provide surveillance of secondary access points. Infrared or supersonic detectors can provide automatic surveillance of closed office spaces. Computers can now even detect voice recognition of words and individual voices. Centralized systems incorporating a small computer are now available to tie together a whole range of safety

and security equipment systems. How much of such elaborate systems is needed for a given project is a matter of judgment. In many cases it may be simpler to anchor down business machines and remove cash or securities from the office space rather than introduce jail-like security measures.

Banks face a special problem because of the omnipresence of cash and the current popularity of bank robbery as a supposedly easy crime. But banks pose a dilemma for the planner and his client. Marketing directions in banking favor an open, welcoming ambience that runs counter to security needs. Many older banks with elaborate teller's cages and easily supervised exit points are more secure than modern, attractively open banks. Technology can offer highly secure arrangements, such as the well-protected teller station, familiar to everyone as drive-in bank windows, but habits and preferences do not seem ready to accept such tight controls. Short of such measures, planning consideration seems to be the best and least costly line of defense. Visibility of the interior space and of the exit routes and construction of exit routes to reduce their attractiveness to potential hold-ups can make a particular bank much less subject to robbery than might otherwise be the case. Scanning cameras to aid in identification of robbers have become routine and seem to be effective, but have had less impact as deterrants than might be expected.

Security of records that are needed for the continued functioning of a business is one more issue that deserves attention. Certain files and documents of a business or organization are always particularly important—that is, irreplaceable and vital to continuing operation. Locking these into a vault or fireproof files is commonplace, but both methods are more troublesome and less secure than duplication and storage at a remote point. Microfilm and computer tape records are compact and offer a way to maintain a second set of records fully available in case of loss, fire damage, or theft of the original records.

All these matters can be dealt with best when new offices are in the planning stage. Office planners have an obligation to bring up the issues of safety and security for review, and their clients should take advantage of the planning period to think through solutions to any current problems and to think ahead to problems that may emerge during the life of the new office. Problems neglected when the project is under construction can be very difficult to deal with fully at some later time.

FURNITURE AND EQUIPMENT

From the point of view of office staff, the things that are of most intimate concern in an office environment are the items of furniture and equipment. However impressive the building, however pleasant the interior spaces, it is the chair, the work surface, the telephone, and possibly the typewriter that are the worker's closest daily companions.

There is a tendency for standards to arise in these matters quite spontaneously. Whatever comes to be regarded as a good desk, chair, or file cabinet is soon made by innumerable different manufacturers. This is a convenient situation for the planner, since any particular maker's product becomes interchangeable with any other. From the design point of view, however, it leads to uniformity and monotony. At one time most office desks were paneled oak; later on, olive-painted steel with rounded corners and linoleum tops became the norm. We have been living through an era of square corners and chrome edges, black paint and (usually imitation) teak.

As in so many other office matters, the arrival of open planning has been a stimulus to new approaches. It is interesting to note that at almost the same moment, starting from an entirely different line of research, Robert Propst's concept of an "Action Office" appeared. As a result of the interaction of these ideas, a whole new generation of office furniture is appearing. This is, unfortunately, accompanied by the usual pattern of imitation, as lesser manufacturers rush to join in the trends suggested by innovative leaders.

Seating has not been subject to equally striking innovation, but technical changes in materials and mechanism has led to some new directions that deserve attention.

Predictions of dramatic changes in other types of equipment, communication devices, business machines, and data storage and retrieval devices do not seem to have been generally realized as yet. The picture phone has not taken over; the data terminal is still much as it was some years ago. Futuristic consoles with screens that can be in instant touch with all human knowledge remain ideas for science fiction rather than everyday office realities.

It is not reasonable to attempt to illustrate a broad range of office furniture and equipment in this book, but this section offers a very limited selection of products that in one way or another embody some interesting ideas about the function of form.

Executive office furniture designed by Warren Platner and produced by Knoll International.

The state of the art as of about 1966. An office designed by Florence Knoll using her own desk and storage components with Mies van der Rohe visitors' chairs. Courtesy Knoll Associates, Inc.

One of the first American systems to respond to the
needs of office landscape is the TAG system produced by
Art Metal (no longer in production).

A desk (above) and an open file unit (right) from the system
developed by Hans Krieks for Designcraft specifically for
use in office landscape spaces.

The Herman Miller system known as "Action Office" was developed by Robert Propst. The use of panels to support work surfaces was not a part of the original approach of office landscape development, but this system has proved to be highly adaptable to open planning.

(Right) A Steelcase system using panels with attached components includes angled binlike shelves for improved paper handling.

The Haller system was developed in Switzerland
and is made in the U.S. by Herman Miller. This highly
adjustable steel structural system supports tops, panels,
files, and other elements to permit very flexible
arrangements with a unique sense of lightness and
openness.

Steelcase 9000 system equipment for office landscape.

An office furniture group designed by Peter Protzman for Herman Miller. Oval chromed steel tubing structure is a consistent characteristic.

Steelcase 9000 system special-purpose work station includes word-processing and CRT units.

(Above) The Stephens System of office furniture was developed by Knoll International in cooperation with Skidmore, Owings, & Merrill specifically for use in the Weyerhaeuser headquarters project (see pp. 148–157). The system is now an available product and is constantly being expanded.

(Right) A secretarial work station, designed by Warren Platner from a system produced by CI Designs. Photograph by Ezra Stoller © ESTO.

A range of swivel office chairs designed by Morrison and Hannah for Knoll International. Seat and back cushions are easily removable, interchangeable components for convenient maintenance.

(Above) Lounge seating by
Morrison and Hannah for
Knoll is part of an exten-
sive system of upholstery.

(Right) Domore Office
Furniture luxury executive
posture chair designed by
Hugh Acton.

Component seating of plastic foam suitable for lobbies and waiting areas by Ray Wilkes for Herman Miller.

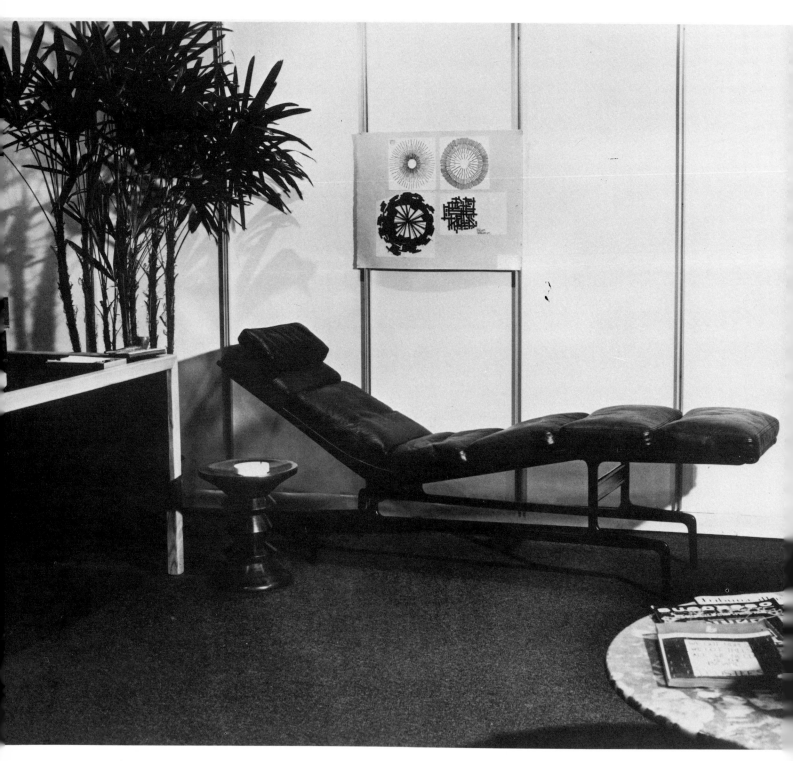

A Charles Eames chaise designed particularly for use in executive offices for brief rest or meditation. Its small scale makes it more office adaptable than most reclining furniture. Courtesy Herman Miller.

INDEX

Edited by Susan Braybrooke, Susan Davis, and Naomi Goldstein
Designed by Jim Craig
Set in 10 point Helvetica by Gerard Associates/Graphic Arts, Inc.